SMART DISCIPLINE

FOURTH EDITION

DISCIPLINE

for the Classroom

Dedicated to Harold and Margaret Koenig—teachers
of unconditional love

SMART DISCIPLINE

FOURTH EDITION

for the Classroom

RESPECT AND COOPERATION RESTORED

LARRY J. KOENIG

CORWIN PRESS
A SAGE Publications Company
Thousand Oaks, CA 91320

Illustrations created by Phil Cangelosi.

For information:

Corwin Press
A Sage Publications Company
2455 Teller Road
Thousand Oaks, California 91320
www.corwinpress.com

Sage Publications Ltd.
1 Oliver's Yard
55 City Road
London EC1Y 1SP
United Kingdom

Sage Publications India Pvt. Ltd.
B 1/I 1 Mohan Cooperative
    Industrial Area
Mathura Road, New Delhi 110 044
India

Sage Publications Asia-Pacific Pte. Ltd.
33 Pekin Street #02-01
Far East Square
Singapore 048763

Printed in the United States of America

Library of Congress Cataloging-in-Publication Data

Koenig, Larry.
Smart discipline for the classroom: Respect and cooperation restored/Larry J. Koenig.—4th ed.
    p. cm.
Includes bibliographical references and index.
ISBN 978-1-4129-5404-4 (cloth)
ISBN 978-1-4129-5405-1 (pbk.)
    1. School discipline—United States. 2. Classroom management—United States. I. Title.

LB3012.2.K64 2008
371.102′4—dc22

2007005862

This book is printed on acid-free paper.

07 08 09 10 11 10 9 8 7 6 5 4 3 2 1

Acquisitions Editor:	Cathy Hernandez
Editorial Assistant:	Megan Bedell
Production Editor:	Melanie Birdsall
Copy Editor:	Renee Willers
Typesetter:	C&M Digitals (P) Ltd.
Proofreader:	Gail Fay
Indexer:	Marilyn Augst
Cover Designer:	Rose Storey
Graphic Designer:	Karine Hovsepian

Contents

Acknowledgments

I owe a debt of gratitude to many people who have contributed to this book in so many ways. Especially, I would like to thank my wife, Nydia. Without her love, patience, inspiration, and hard work, *Smart Discipline for the Classroom* would not exist.

PUBLISHER'S ACKNOWLEDGEMENTS

Corwin Press gratefully acknowledges the contributions of the following reviewers:

Jane D. Adair
Resource Specialist
Long Beach Polytechnic High
  School
Long Beach, CA

Roxie Ahlbrecht
Second-Grade Teacher
Robert Frost Elementary School
Sioux Falls, SD

Carrie Jane Carpenter
Language Arts Teacher
Deschutes Edge Charter School
Redmond, OR

Sharon J. Damore
Assistant Professor of Education
DePaul University
Chicago, IL

Arlene C. Miguel
Principal
Hampden Meadows School
Barrington, RI

Gina Segobiano
Superintendent
Harmony-Emge School
  District #175
Belleville, IL

Paulette Tetteris-Woosley
Assistant Principal
Wallburg Elementary
Winston-Salem, NC

Kathleen Thomas
Marketing Education Teacher
Caesar Rodney High School
Camden, DE

About the Author

 **Larry J. Koenig,** a nationally known authority in the areas of discipline and parenting, is the president and CEO of Smart Discipline LLC. Early in his career, he worked extensively with children and adolescents in a variety of settings, including classrooms, youth development centers, and psychiatric hospitals.

While working with students and classroom teachers throughout the United States, Dr. Koenig developed the Smart Discipline System. Using this system, he has trained thousands of teachers in strategies for building self-esteem in young people and in classroom discipline. The demand for this program continues to grow as parents and teachers alike have become increasingly challenged by the task of teaching children. In addition to training educators, Dr. Koenig offers ongoing consultation to ensure that the program is implemented effectively.

Dr. Koenig is the creator of the nationally acclaimed Smart Discipline for Parents program and the president of the North American Society for Parent Training and Development. Hospitals, television stations, and schools nationwide have sponsored this program for over 20 years. In this seminar, he focuses on the two topics about which parents most want information: self-esteem and discipline. He also trains school counselors in Smart Discipline for Parents so they can train parents in the system throughout the school year as needs arise.

Dr. Koenig is a recognized media personality, public speaker, and humorist. For two years, he has done a weekly parenting series for the ABC affiliate (WBRZ) in Baton Rouge, Louisiana. He is also frequently interviewed by television and radio stations throughout America. It is often said at his public appearances that he has the unique ability to talk about exactly what is going on in today's classrooms and to give both meaningful and practical advice.

Dr. Koenig lives with his family in Baton Rouge, Louisiana. He may be contacted by telephone at 1-800-208-0807 or via his Web site at www.smart discipline.org.

Introduction

The purpose of this book is to assist teachers in developing a personal plan of action to handle discipline in the classroom. Because of the plethora of misbehaviors in today's classroom, not having an effective discipline plan will thwart an instructor's goal of teaching. If you are a teacher, this needs no explanation. You already know how disruptive students can be.

Back in the dark ages of the 1950s and 1960s, all a teacher needed to be effective was a good lesson plan. Now, that is not enough. A plan for handling behavior is also necessary. And it must be one that can do the following:

- Be individualized to fit each instructor's teaching style and personality
- Prevent misbehaviors and encourage cooperation
- Motivate a student to stop disruptive behaviors
- Motivate a student to want to learn
- Be quick and easy to use

Smart Discipline for the Classroom encompasses these goals. Also, you will find Smart Discipline strategies to be adaptable to the different needs and personalities of children. More important, the system provides for "Plan A" and "Plan B" strategies that are progressive and always provide a "next step."

Plan A strategies are ones that take seconds to implement. They are quick and easy methods for both strengthening the teacher-student relationship and gaining immediate cooperation.

Plan B strategies take more time to implement but are designed to turn around the attitudes and behaviors of specific children. Most frequently, they will be used when Plan A methods have not produced satisfactory results.

All the strategies are presented in a logical progression. However, that does not mean they have to be used in that order—quite the contrary. The Smart Discipline strategies are designed with flexibility in mind. It is my hope that you will be able to pick and choose methods that will fit your teaching style and that will work in a given situation with a particular child.

WHO CAN BENEFIT FROM THIS BOOK?

Smart Discipline for the Classroom originally was written with teachers in mind. However, over the past several years, a diversified audience has come to use the information. The list seems to be ever growing and now includes

- School counselors
- Principals
- Teacher educators
- School secretaries
- School nurses
- Cafeteria workers
- Bus drivers
- Coaches
- Sunday school teachers
- Therapists
- Alcohol and drug counselors
- Foster parents
- Stepparents
- Police officers

This is a long list, but not a surprising one. All the people represented have a common need to relate to young people in a way that will motivate them to cooperate and accept guidance. In today's world, it is indeed a difficult task to gain the necessary cooperation from students of all ages—even young ones. The fact is that all of us who work with students are finding the task an increasing challenge.

We need all the help we can get to successfully meet this challenge and to guide children down a path toward success in life. The strategies and principles described in these pages are the stepping stones to meeting this important task with confidence.

THREE PRACTICAL CONSIDERATIONS

I have presented the information contained in this book to groups of teachers all across America. Each time I do so, the feedback is overwhelmingly positive. However, several teachers in each location typically bring up one of three problems that they view as insurmountable. They describe the problems with statements such as the following:

Although I like the ideas, I don't have the time to use them. All of my time is taken up with trying to control the class, teaching, and completing paperwork.

My problem is that I have too many students for these ideas to be practical.

I've got a student in my class whose behavior is really rotten. I've tried everything and nothing works.

Because these issues are recurring and very real, I would like to address each one at the outset.

Time is an issue for every teacher. And there always seem to be more and more things for teachers to do that take away from teaching time. Smart

Discipline is not one of them, however. The effort invested in implementing these strategies will prevent discipline problems. This saves time in the long run.

Having an overload of students is also common. Some teachers have 100 or more students at a time to deal with in a study hall or cafeteria seating. So, "How do I discipline a large group?" is a legitimate question.

The answer is, "You don't." Trying to discipline a group of any size is a losing battle. To be successful with discipline, it needs to be done on a one-to-one basis. And in reality, you will only need to use Smart Discipline with a few students. Get them cooperating with you, and the rest will follow suit.

Last, there is the problem of what to do with the student who is resisting your best efforts (and driving you up the wall). One of the main reasons I have included a large variety of discipline strategies is because of this very problem.

Being successful with the most difficult discipline problems requires persistent, positive effort with a diverse assortment of techniques (F. Jones, 1987). With every student, something will work. For those of us who have chosen to work with students, it is our challenge to find out what that something is.

It is my hope that within these pages you will find what is needed to meet this challenge and to put your students on the "superhighway toward success in school and in life."

WHAT *SMART DISCIPLINE FOR THE CLASSROOM* COVERS

Smart Discipline for the Classroom covers the following topics:

- Disruptive behaviors and their causes
- The usual approaches to discipline and their drawbacks
- The commonsense principles on which Smart Discipline is based
- Prevention strategies
- Intervention strategies to motivate a student to stop disruptive behaviors and adopt productive behaviors
- ADHD—information and strategies that work
- Designing a customized Smart Discipline plan to fit your needs
- Effective strategies for gaining parental involvement and support

The Smart Discipline Advantages

- Retains teacher's authority
- Provides quick and easy solutions
- Adapts to different students
- Helps teachers stay calm and in charge
- Builds self-esteem
- Adapts to individual teaching styles
- Fosters behaviors conducive to learning
- Steers clear of power struggles
- Prevents misconduct
- Uses ADHD strategies

- Offers progressive steps
- Motivates students to pay attention
- Stops disruptive behaviors
- Builds strong teacher-student relationships
- Helps students successfully learn
- Helps teachers successfully educate
- Motivates respect for teachers, self, and others

As you can see, a lot is promised. The ultimate promise is that you will be able to take your plan into the classroom and achieve the results you need and want. If you cannot do this, I have failed in my purpose. But, in teaching and in learning, failure only comes to those who give up.

So, never—never—never give up!

Good luck!

Misbehaviors and Their Causes 1

Teaching is tough. Today's classrooms are populated with students exhibiting a wide variety of disruptive behaviors. Some examples follow. You may think of others.

_____ 1. Shouting out	_____ 23. Stealing
_____ 2. Passing notes	_____ 24. Hitting
_____ 3. Cheating	_____ 25. Sleeping
_____ 4. Making threats	_____ 26. Teasing
_____ 5. Committing violent acts	_____ 27. Playing pranks
_____ 6. Swearing	_____ 28. Insulting
_____ 7. Talking back, sassing	_____ 29. Displaying negative attitude
_____ 8. Wandering out of seat	_____ 30. Outbursts of anger
_____ 9. Throwing things	_____ 31. Indifference
_____ 10. Skipping school	_____ 32. Clowning
_____ 11. Defying authority	_____ 33. Arguing
_____ 12. Hyperactivity	_____ 34. Talking
_____ 13. Not following directions	_____ 35. Borrowing without asking
_____ 14. Crying	_____ 36. Showing bad manners
_____ 15. Interrupting	_____ 37. Being sarcastic
_____ 16. Complaining constantly	_____ 38. Being inattentive
_____ 17. Lying	_____ 39. Dressing inappropriately
_____ 18. Being late	_____ 40. Daydreaming
_____ 19. Throwing temper tantrums	_____ Other:_____
_____ 20. Chewing gum	_____ Other:_____
_____ 21. Being disrespectful	_____ Other:_____
_____ 22. Not completing work	_____ Other:_____

That is quite a list, right? It is almost overwhelming when you consider that a teacher might have several students misbehaving in the same class. No wonder it is tough to teach sometimes. (Good thing we have many highly dedicated teachers in the United States.)

Because we will need it later to customize a Smart Discipline plan for you, please list five behaviors that disrupt your class most frequently.

1. _____

2. _____

3. _____

4. _____

5. _____

Next, list the three most difficult behaviors for you to handle. They may be the same or different from those you listed above.

1. _____

2. _____

3. _____

CAUSES OF MISBEHAVIORS

When I conduct workshops around the country, a question frequently asked is, "Why do you think there are so many more problems with behavior in school today compared with the way it was 20 or 30 years ago?" If I turn the question around and ask the workshop group what they think, there is a general consensus that two conditions are primarily to blame:

1. The breakup of the family

2. The lack of parental involvement and support in and for the schools

Undeniably, these two conditions have dramatically changed over the years, and most certainly, behavior in the schools has been adversely affected.

But there are many other maladies that affect behavior and should also be taken into account.

This, too, is quite a list. All kinds of things can cause a child to act out in the classroom. It is important to know this so that we do not take a child's misbehavior personally. If we take it personally, we will tend to respond emotionally rather than logically. Responding emotionally usually only makes the situation worse (more about this later). We need to be aware that on any given day any student might act out in reaction to a personal problem and that we cannot fix all of his or her problems.

_____	1. Low self-esteem	_____	16. Fetal alcohol syndrome
_____	2. Drug abuse	_____	17. Underachievement syndrome
_____	3. ADD and ADHD	_____	18. Poverty
_____	4. Dysfunctional families	_____	19. Attachment disorder
_____	5. Childhood depression	_____	20. Sociopathology
_____	6. Child abuse	_____	21. Prejudice
_____	7. Sexual abuse	_____	22. Anxiety
_____	8. Oppositional disorder	_____	23. Eating disorders
_____	9. Alcoholism	_____	24. Dyslexia
_____	10. Gangs	_____	25. Negative peer pressure
_____	11. Family violence	_____	26. Steroid abuse
_____	12. Personality conflicts	_____	27. Loss of hope
_____	13. Puberty	_____	28. Television sex and violence
_____	14. Verbal abuse	_____	29. Negative role models
_____	15. Community violence	_____	Other: _____

I THOUGHT YOU WERE GOING TO MAKE A LIST OF ONLY THOSE BEHAVIORS THAT ARE **MOST** IN NEED OF CHANGE.

I DID. THIS IS IT.

A list of 5 or 10 behaviors is a manageable number.

The good news is this: We can gain a student's cooperation anyway! In the next chapter, though, we will look at the usual ways we use to correct behavior. We will also explore their drawbacks.

As much as we would like to think our students will "just say no," sometimes they do not. Consequently, moods and behaviors in the classroom are adversely affected.

Usual Discipline Methods and Their Drawbacks 2

The discipline methods discussed in this section are the most prevalent ones used by our generation. They were not taught to us in school. For the most part, the discipline techniques we favor are the ones our parents and teachers used with us.

The funny thing is, we continue using them in the face of the evidence that

- Often, they did not work with us when we were growing up.
- Often, they do not produce the expected results when we use them.

That we continue doing what does not work is an interesting phenomenon. Einstein once said that the definition of insanity is expecting different results from the same behavior.

We continue ineffective behaviors for several reasons:

- Behaviors learned through observation and mimicking become deeply ingrained.
- Habits are tough to break (even in the face of profound logic that we should do so).
- Ineffective methods sometimes work, and this leads us to believe they will work again if we are persistent.

The underlying problem is that sometimes the methods can both severely damage our relations with the child and even cause further acting out.

As we look at each of the most common discipline techniques, we will also look at why using them can work at cross-purposes with the goals of discipline. The goals of discipline are to motivate a student to do the following:

- Stop disruptive behaviors
- Adopt productive behaviors
- Have a desire to cooperate

Method: Lectures

Example: "Brad, I saw you throw your pencil at Kenny. I can't believe you would do such a stupid thing. Don't you realize you could hit him in the eye and blind him? How would you like it if someone poked your eye out with a pencil?"

Problems: Lecturing provides an emotional release for the lecturer but is usually ineffective in preventing further disruptive behaviors. Here is why. When a child is deciding whether or not to misbehave, three questions quickly pass through his or her mind:

- Will I get caught?
- Will I get punished?
- Will I get out of it somehow?

All kids think they will not get caught. However, we really get into trouble when a student is answering the second question by thinking, "Even if I do get caught, I'm not going to get punished. Oh sure, I'll get yelled at and lectured to, but I won't really get punished." If a child is answering the question in this fashion, he or she will not likely be motivated to curtail future misbehaviors.

Also, when we lecture, the child may well feel put down or embarrassed. If that happens, watch out. This can cause a child to take his or her resulting anger and resentment out on you. This child's retaliation can lead to an ongoing battle that only escalates. If that happens, you know lecturing is not working for you or the child.

Please note: Later chapters will reveal methods that work.

Method: Threats

Example: "Phyllis, you better straighten your act up, young lady, or you'll really be in trouble."

Problems: There are several drawbacks to threats. They include the following:

- Threats are often made in anger, a fact that usually fosters angry responses.
- Power struggles that destroy cooperation may result.
- Most threats are never carried out, and kids know it.

Method: Rewards

Example: "Jerry, if you stay in your seat all morning, I will get or let you _____."

Problems: Rewards can motivate some children to behave on a short-term basis. However, no matter what reward you use to fill in the blank, you will sooner or later run into these difficulties:

- The child may decide he or she no longer wants the reward and so may have no incentive to comply.
- The child may come to expect rewards that you will be neither able nor willing to provide.
- A reward system takes a lot of time to maintain.
- Research clearly concludes that for rewards to be effective, they must be (a) immediate and (b) intermittent. Try to juggle this and teach at the same time!

In some settings, a reward system can be highly effective. The dilemma is that the variables needed are difficult to control in a classroom. Trying to do so often leaves both the teacher and the child frustrated.

Method: Punishment

Example: "I'm tired of you being late for class all the time. I've warned you enough and given you plenty of chances to be on time. Because you still haven't, you will have to _____."

Problems: Providing consequences for misbehaving can be highly effective. However, to make those consequences provide the results you want, certain guidelines must be followed. These will be discussed in Chapter 4. In the meantime, let us look at the drawbacks if the guidelines are not followed.

- Punishment causes some students to want revenge. Everyone loses then.
- Students may say, "I don't care" or "So what?"
- Students may manipulate us not to enforce the consequences. When this happens, we are in danger of setting a child up to think, "Even if I do get caught and get punished, I can crawfish my way out of it." Not good!

As human beings, we are known to be inconsistent with punishment. We will punish one time and not the next. We will even punish one child and not another. This can cause further problems in the classroom if students become vocal over inconsistencies and possible favoritism.

For discipline to work in the classroom, a well-thought-out system of rules and consequences must be in place. Impulsive and arbitrary punishment does not work. In fact, we can do more harm than good by punishing on the spur of the moment.

Method: Comparisons

Example: "Everyone, pay attention to how Jennifer is sitting quietly at her desk with her assignment done. Cindy, I want you especially to pay attention. If you would just act more like Jennifer, you would do a lot better in my class."

Problems: Some professionals in the areas of education and psychology advocate teachers' drawing attention to a child exhibiting the desired behavior and asking other students to follow suit. Sounds like a good idea, but

- The vast majority of kids hate to be publicly singled out for model behavior. It causes them to get labeled as nerds or teacher's pets. In short, they get rejected. When this happens, they try not to repeat the behaviors that got them singled out.
- The natural response to being asked to be like someone else is, "I'm not that person. I don't want to be that person. And I will not act like that person, no matter what."

When a younger sibling of a highly successful student comes to school, unfortunate and frequent comparisons occur. As comparisons continue to be made, the younger child commonly tries to establish his or her own identity by acting contrary to the older sibling. Or the child may even give up trying to succeed in school, thinking, "No matter how much effort I put in, I won't be able to achieve the success level of my big brother or sister, so why even try?" This, of course, is loser logic, but it happens. And it especially happens when "well-intended" comparisons are made.

Method: Anger

Anger does not sound like a discipline method, does it? But we use it like one.

Example: "You've got me really mad now. I can't wait to get hold of your parents. I'm going to give them an earful. I hope you get grounded for a month! Now, go back to your seat and stay there until I tell you to leave."

Problems: Angry outbursts work for us sometimes. At least, they can frequently get immediate results. The sheer force of energy in the emotion can frighten a child into compliance. However, we must watch out for the aftereffects:

- Anger begets anger. You can expect an angry response at some point. How it comes back to you will be destructive. You can count on it. Unfortunately, you will not know when or where it will manifest itself.
- There is a direct relationship between anger and reason. The more anger in an exchange, the less reason.

- Some kids love to "push a teacher's buttons" to get the teacher angry. They think it is funny. Worse, they perceive the teacher to be out of control and themselves in control.
- When we respond with anger, we sometimes say and do things we later regret (but cannot take back). Being human, you know what I mean. It happens to all of us.

Method: Criticism, or Reverse Psychology

Example: "You know what your problem is, Greg? Your problem is that you're just plain lazy. I told you to have your homework done by this morning. But you didn't do it, did you? No, you didn't. The problem with you is that you're just plain lazy, and you are never going to amount to anything."

Problems: We learned this technique from our parents' generation. It is based on a theory that reasons as follows: "If you point out evidence to another person that he or she has a character defect, the person will change." In our generation, we call this logic *reverse psychology.* It is a slight variation on the belief that if you tell people that they cannot do something, then that will cause them to do it.

All of us can cite numerous examples of how our use of criticism caused someone to change his or her behavior. Sure, it can work, but using criticism is playing with dynamite for the following reasons:

- Criticism destroys relationships. Human beings, young and old, hate to be criticized. It makes us angry and resentful, and it makes us criticize right back.
- Criticism can cause another person to refuse to cooperate with us. It even riles feelings of hate, especially in students with low self-esteem.
- Criticism cultivates and reinforces negative beliefs. When we point out someone's negative behavior and ascribe it to a character fault, we may well cause that person to believe that is "just the way I am." The person then continues to act that way.

When we use criticism, we do so because of a good intention to help a person change or because we are angry at the person. Either way, criticism can erode relationships and self-esteem.

Method: Corporal Punishment

Example: Student misbehaves and the teacher sends the student to the principal's office. The principal spanks the child.

Problems: In some ways, I hate to even broach the issue of corporal punishment. It is a no-win situation because people have strong opinions on both sides of the issue. Their minds are already made up.

I am against it for the following reasons:

- If you spank a child, you run the risk of making an enemy for life, an enemy who will seek revenge.
- Some kids could not care less if they get spanked. In fact, they prefer it. It lets them off the hook by leading them to think, "I can do anything I want because even if I get caught, the worst that will happen is a spanking."
- Corporal punishment is now illegal in many states.

No matter how we personally view it, the whole issue of corporal punishment is a dead issue. Society in general no longer condones it, and school boards will not allow it. These stances are not likely to change in the foreseeable future.

Method: The Vulcan Pinch

Example: Student acts out, and the teacher maneuvers around behind the student to execute a pinch of the trapezoid muscle.

Problems: I just know a number of you are thinking: "Who would do such a thing in this day and age?" Others are thinking, "What's the big deal? It's quick and easy, and it works." If you are an advocate of the Vulcan Pinch, consider the following:

- The infliction of physical pain causes anger, feelings of hate, and a desire for revenge. In no way will it instill in a child a positive desire to cooperate with you.
- A well-intentioned, motivational pinch can cause the loss of a job and create a lawsuit to boot.

The answer to the question, "Who would do such a thing in this day and age?" is, "Lots of us." But we need to stop it.

Method: Commands

Example: "Go back to your seat right now! And take off those sunglasses immediately!"

Problems: The older the student, the less likely this will work. You might get away with barking an order at a primary student, but when a child attains the age of 10, watch out! As a result of making commands, you are likely to generate problems such as the following:

- A student may respond with, "Make me." However you respond at this point, whether you enter into a power struggle or back down, you will lose, and so will the student. (Why power struggles must be avoided at all costs will be dealt with extensively later.)

- The student may respond with, "Why?" Two likely responses to this are either "Because I said so," or "The reason why." Students resent the first response and argue with the second. Some kids, by the way, love nothing better than to lure a teacher into a good argument. Once it starts, everyone loses.

- The student may respond to your command by ignoring you and acting as if you did not even say anything. We then repeat the command more loudly, an act that begets a blank stare from the student (that says, "Who, me?"). This aggravates us to the point where we may say something like, "Yes, you, you big dummy!" From here, there is no good way to go.

One thing common to adults and kids alike is their dislike for being ordered to do something. We all resist this approach to some degree. Try it with a strong-willed and oppositional child, and it will end in disaster. More about how to avoid this later.

You can take your chances with criticism, but you will always lose.

Method: Note to Parents

Example:

> Dear Mrs. Greene,
>
> Your daughter Mandy is being disruptive in class, and her homework assignments are consistently incomplete. Please do whatever you can to rectify this situation. Please let me know if you have questions.
>
> Sincerely,
> Mrs. Bunker

Problems: Notes can be highly effective, but there are several pitfalls. They include the following:

- The note may never get home.
- If Mrs. Greene is an all-American mother, she will ask Mandy what is going on. If Mandy is an all-American girl, she will explain to her mother that it is not her fault. She will blame the other kids and say, "But the real problem is the teacher—she doesn't like me and is always picking on me."
- Chances are that the parents will give Mandy a good lecture, and that will be the end of it.

If your notes are not getting results, it is probably because of one of these pitfalls.

Method: Principal's Office

Example: Student acts out in class and is asked to go to the principal's office. Teacher sends along a note that says:

> Charles has been disruptive in class all period. He has been uncooperative and disrespectful. This includes being out of his seat, talking, and using vulgarity.
>
> Thank you,
> Mrs. Simms

Problems: One common drawback in sending a student to the principal's office is that the whole class gets the message that you are not the ultimate authority, the principal is. As we will see later, it is possible to get the principal involved in the solution process without giving up authority. In the meantime, before you send a student to the principal, as in my example, consider these issues:

- Children lie. It is a fact, and they will paint their own picture of reality, especially when confronted by a principal.
- It is difficult for a principal to effectively handle a situation without knowing what actually happened.
- The principal's resolution will be questioned when the student returns to class. The offender will be asked by friends, "What happened?" to which the child will respond, "Principal didn't do nothing to me; it was no big deal!" Inevitably, you will lose face with the class.

There are several powerful ways to solve behavioral problems by involving the principal while the teacher remains the authority figure for the students. These will be dealt with in detail in Chapter 5.

Before we get to these strategies and others, in the next chapter we will discuss the principles on which the strategies are founded, plus some highly effective prevention principles.

Commonsense Principles of Smart Discipline 3

This chapter will deal with the principles behind the prevention and intervention strategies that follow. I call them *commonsense principles* because they make sense to me. They evolved out of my work with thousands of kids all over America, in a variety of settings: classrooms, family counseling, reform schools, psychiatric hospitals, and my Up With Youth program.

Although these principles make a lot of sense to me, you will have to make up your own mind. None of them, you will find, are new. All have been passed down to us through the ages in one fashion or another.

Principle 1: Change Happens Both Quickly and Slowly

Some students will respond immediately to discipline methods. Some respond so quickly and completely that what you are doing may seem like magic. Others respond so slowly that we conclude that our methods are not working.

As a general rule, we should commit to a plan of action for at least a month before we give up and try something else. Remember that more is accomplished in life through sheer persistence than anything else.

Principle 2: Methods That Work for Some Students Will Not Work for Others

Kids, as you know, are different. It is surprising when an approach that works wonders with one child does not work with another. The common human response to this is irritation. It aggravates us when children are unresponsive to our positive efforts. I think it might be because a lack of response or a negative response makes us feel rejected or unappreciated.

Whatever your feelings when your efforts fail, they are natural and to be expected. The most common reaction is to respond negatively to the child. This is also the most common mistake. A more positive strategy is to be ready with another positive approach.

Principle 3: A Well-Thought-Out Personal Discipline Plan Is Essential

In today's schools, some things are for certain. One is that some students will misbehave. Unfortunately, the number of students who misbehave is growing, as is the variety and severity of misbehaviors.

Not having a well-thought-out plan for how to handle these misbehaviors is as foolhardy as teaching without a lesson plan. Or, if you prefer, it is like going out to coach a game without a game plan. The results of either are less than satisfactory.

Confronting misbehavior without a discipline plan will also yield less than satisfactory results. Without a plan, we naturally resort to the discipline methods with which we were raised. Many of these, as described in Chapter 2, not only do not work but actually foster more misbehavior.

Having a well-thought-out discipline plan will produce both the desired results and a feeling of confidence (Boynton & Boynton, 2005). Suffice it to say, having a sound discipline plan will help you attain your ultimate goal: that is, to teach!

Principle 4: Adults Give Positive Students Positive Feedback and Negative Students Negative Feedback

Although there are exceptions, for the most part, we are conditioned to respond to positive children with delightful and encouraging comments. When this happens between teacher and student, several things occur:

- The child's desire to cooperate with the teacher increases.
- The child's desire to learn from the teacher increases.
- The teacher helps the child believe that the child "has what it takes" to be successful in school.

Unfortunately, we are conditioned to respond to negative children with sometimes demeaning and discouraging remarks (Kottler, 2002). We do so because their behavior is irritating to us and because we believe that by pointing out the "errors of their ways," we will motivate them to change. When teachers take this approach, the following are likely to occur:

- The child's desire to cooperate with the teacher decreases.
- The child's desire to learn from the teacher decreases.
- The teacher helps the child believe that the child "doesn't have what it takes" to be successful in school.

Someday soon (maybe today will be the day), we will realize that negative responses to children only perpetuate negative behavior. To be honest, many of us have realized this. However, we continue responding negatively because we have been conditioned to react in this way and have not yet found a new approach that works for us.

Principle 5: Using the Same Discipline Methods Over and Over Will Yield the Same Results; Therefore, If You Wish to Change the Results, You Must Change Discipline Methods

This, I know, sounds rather elementary. However, as humans, we often get stuck in a rut. What happens is that we try something with a student one time, and it works. The next 10 times it does not, but we keep it up because we reason that if it worked once, it should work again.

When we are unsuccessful in getting a child to modify or change a behavior, we do something rather silly: we blame the child. Or we blame the parents, or the socioeconomic conditions, or TV, or the phase of the moon, for that matter.

Although we need to give strategies a fair chance to work, sometimes, in order to engineer positive results, we need to change discipline strategies.

Principle 6: The More a Student Acts Out, the More the Student Will Benefit From a Well-Thought-Out, Positive Plan of Action

Typically, children who act out at school are getting negative feedback and criticism heaped on them both at school and at home. When this happens, students usually respond with anger or depression, neither of which is conducive to learning (Labelee, 2004).

What a shock it is to a negative student to have someone consistently respond with a positive approach. In fact, having one teacher do so can sometimes totally turn a student around.

Principle 7: Students Will Often Act Worse in Response to Positive Approaches

There is a reason for this: Children are like a lot of grown-ups. That is, they like things to remain the same because they know what to expect and how to respond. Changes, therefore, frequently cause harsh and negative reactions meant to result in a return to old and familiar patterns.

Also, kids like to conduct their own research. They like to test things out to see if the change in response is "for real" or not. We must expect negative reactions and pass their test by responding with positive interventions, even in the face of negative feedback from the student.

Although we need to change the discipline techniques that are not working with a particular student, we must resist the natural urge to respond negatively to a student who responds negatively to our positive efforts. Rather, when we have determined after a couple of weeks that a particular strategy is not working, we need to be ready with another constructive approach.

In the meantime, anticipate negative reactions, and keep your responses positive!

Principle 8: Behaviors That We Pay Attention to Are Reinforced

This explains a mystery. It gives us the reason why we often fail miserably when we try so hard to change a child's behavior.

What I mean is this: All children thrive on attention. And all children try to garner attention through positive behavior and achievements. Some are successful, and some are not. Those who are not successful through positive means learn very quickly to get attention by acting out. The attention they get, of course, simply motivates them to continue acting out.

Even though we understand this and have talked about it among ourselves many times, we get sucked right into participating in this negative cycle anyway. The only way out of it is to follow the Boy Scout motto and "be prepared" with a positive plan of action.

Please note: Have patience. We are going to start putting together just such a plan in the next chapter.

Principle 9: People Treat Us the Way We Treat Them

We are all familiar with this principle. It is also one we teach to children. We tell them, "If you want people to be nice to you, then you must be nice to them."

This is a principle that we put into practice, for the most part. Unfortunately, we tend to throw it out the window when someone is being nasty to us. Nastiness causes us to be mean right back. Once we do so, a negative cycle gets set into motion that is tough to break. Maybe this is why someone very wise once advised, "Turn the other cheek."

When we turn the other cheek, we need to be ready with a positive response, one that bespeaks kindness, concern, and compassion. The payoff will come in setting in motion a positive cycle that also will be hard to break.

Principle 10: Some Kids Irritate Us

The opposite is also true. Some kids delight us. Of course, we get along well with these kids. We just seem to hit it off with them. Discipline with these kids is rarely a problem. For one thing, they want to behave for us. We also overlook minor indiscretions because we like them.

Woe unto the child, though, who irritates us. With this child, we typically are hypercritical and unforgiving. Some would say it is because these children are displaying the flaws that we dislike (or hate) in ourselves.

Whatever the reason, it is beneficial to face up to our humanness and realize that some kids will always rub us the wrong way. Benefits are achieved by allowing ourselves to be human while purposely deciding to resolve these personality conflicts with a positive plan of action.

Principle 11: Anger Blocks Learning

Think about this for a moment: Would you buy something from someone with whom you are angry? Not on your life. In fact, we will do whatever it takes to avoid doing business with that person. Kids are the same way with their teachers. No way will a student "buy" what the teacher is selling if he or she is angry with the teacher.

What the child will do instead is fill his or her mind with the following:

- Thoughts of revenge
- Thoughts of how unfair the teacher is
- Plans of how he or she can convince everyone else how wicked the teacher is

When the student's mind is busy with these thoughts, the learning process becomes solidly blocked.

Later chapters will reveal ways to both prevent and overcome anger.

Principle 12: Teaching Is Not a Popularity Contest

I mention this because I can predict that at this point some teachers are thinking, "I'm not teaching to make friends with my students" and "Why should I have to walk around on eggshells so I don't hurt anyone's feelings?"

The reason is that if it is your goal to teach, then you must pay attention to your students and develop a positive relationship between yourself and them. Students will not learn from or cooperate with a teacher whom they perceive to be unfriendly, uncaring, and disrespectful (Cummings, 2000).

No, teaching is not a popularity contest, but it is a fact that the stronger the teacher-student relationship, the more the student will (a) behave, (b) learn from the teacher, and (c) accept correction (Marzano, 2003). Knowing this, we can put it to work for us so that we will be more effective teachers.

Principle 13: Issues Should Be Dealt With on a Feeling Level Outside the Classroom

For the past couple of decades, we have been taught to resolve difficulties with other people by expressing our feelings. My generation (the baby boomers) has not learned how to do this very well. We need to keep practicing until we get it right. Repressed feelings have a way of coming back to haunt us.

But as with everything, there is a time and a place. The place not to express negative feelings is in the classroom—at least not at the time we are feeling them. When we are in the midst of a raw emotion, we tend to say and do things we regret later. And we tend to spark emotional responses in the person with whom we are communicating. When this happens, nobody wins. Everyone loses.

Our upbeat moods uplift those around us.

A far more productive strategy is to "stay in your head" and deal with conflicts on an intellectual level in the classroom. The expression of feelings should be confined to a one-on-one basis, away from other students—after everyone has calmed down. How feelings can be used effectively with students will be dealt with under the segment titled "Strategy: Deliver 'I' Messages" later in this book (page 67).

Principle 14: Children Are Purveyors of Misinformation

This is a polite way of stating the fact that many children lie on occasion, which is not to say that all children are liars.

The point is this: We can expect children to lie to protect themselves. Therefore, we can expect them to lie when we ask them questions about their involvement in misdeeds. It is only natural for them to do so as an act of self-preservation.

Please note: Yes, I know there are some kids who are exceptionally honest.

Although we realize that children are prone to lying, we adults do an absurd thing: We question them, or we send them to the principal or home with a note, expecting them to tell the truth. Of course, they often do not tell the truth. We then do something even more absurd: We get angry at them for lying.

We need to find ways to confront negative behavior while encouraging honesty.

Principle 15: Power Struggles Must Be Avoided at All Costs

Power struggles between teachers and students always end badly. The older the student, the worse the outcome. Today, these power struggles are apt to end in the student committing defiant acts, such as any of the following:

- Swearing
- Hitting
- Stabbing
- Shooting

That is the bad news. The good news is that there are numerous ways to gain a student's cooperation without getting into a power struggle (Nelson, 1999). All of the discipline strategies in Chapters 4, 5, 6, 7, and 8 focus on accomplishing just that.

Principle 16: Words Are Powerful

Words are powerful because they are the seeds from which beliefs grow. Let me explain by describing the step-by-step process of how beliefs are formed.

When children are growing up, they are trying to answer a subconscious question that goes something like this: "Who am I? What makes me different from everyone around me?" As children seek answers, they listen to information about themselves from other people. As children obtain information, they draw conclusions about themselves and look around for evidence to support the conclusions (and normally find it). Children then integrate the conclusions into their self-talk and belief system. Once this happens, children act according to their beliefs.

Here is an example. A teacher hands a math paper back to a student and says, "Look, Brad, you got an A. I think you have a natural ability for math." Brad, of course, feels pretty good about this, so he studies his math even harder and ends up with an A on his report card. Quite naturally, he thinks, "My teacher is right; I am good in math." He then continues to affirm his belief by taking additional math courses in order to improve his math skills.

It is as simple as that. A teacher can point out something to a student once and give life to a belief that will last a lifetime. Words are that powerful!

Principle 17: Students Act According to Their Beliefs

Once individuals adopt beliefs, the beliefs guide both their behaviors and their decisions. Trying to get a person to act contrary to a belief is difficult at best.

This explains why traditional approaches to modifying behavior often fail. If, for instance, a child picks up a belief like, "I don't have what it takes to be successful in school," then it does not matter how wonderful a system of rules, rewards, and consequences you have. You will not be successful in implementing the learning process in that child.

A child who believes that he or she cannot be successful in school usually seeks out the company of other students who have decided the same thing. They support one another in the belief that "school is for nerds and doesn't matter anyway." This belief frees them to devote 100 percent of their time to being disruptive in the classroom.

What a mess this causes for the teacher! These students now have absolutely nothing to lose. Threats of punishment and banishment become a big joke to them.

To reach these kids, radical steps must be taken to instill beliefs that they have what it takes to be successful in school and that success in school will enable them to get what they want out of life (Dreikurs, 1991). Helping a student adopt these two beliefs is probably one of the best things we can ever do for the student. Without these, the child is lost, and so are all of our efforts to guide that child's behavior in the classroom.

Principle 18: Success Is Dependent on Encouragement

Every single human being needs encouragement. Without it, we give up. Unfortunately, students with significant behavior problems overwhelmingly receive negative and discouraging feedback. After a time, they give up.

When I talk about this, many teachers say, "But what are we to do when so much of this negativity is being heaped on the child at home?" The answer is, "A lot." A teacher should never underestimate his or her potential to positively affect a student's life.

I meet people every single day who attribute their success in life to teachers who took the time and effort to encourage them. The less support a child is receiving at home, the greater the impact of a teacher's encouragement.

Self-esteem is molded mainly by feedback from adults.

Principle 19: "An Ounce of Prevention Is Worth a Pound of Cure" (Ben Franklin)

In reference to classroom discipline, this famous quote holds true. Once a child enters into a pattern of misbehavior, it takes a concentrated effort to turn that around.

The good news is that disruptive behavior can be prevented. It can be thwarted with friendliness, concern, and respect. When students perceive civil treatment from a teacher, they will bend over backwards to cooperate (Mendler & Curwin, 1999). And they will even provide peer pressure for others in the class to follow suit.

The more effort put into developing teacher-student relationships, the less effort will be needed to correct misbehavior (Marzano, 2003). Because prevention is critical, the whole next chapter will be devoted to the specifics of how this can be accomplished.

Principle 20: Teachers Have a Powerful Effect on People's Lives

Behind every single successful human being, there exists a group of dedicated teachers. They not only taught the student but also provided discipline, motivation, and encouragement. Teachers provide the foundation on which success is built.

I mention this not just as a positive stroke but as a fact for teachers to keep in mind when the going gets tough with a particular student. The more negative and defiant the student, the more he or she stands to benefit from a persistently positive approach from the teacher. A positive stance can literally save a child from oblivion.

The rule to keep in mind is this: The more irritated, aggravated, or hopeless a student makes you feel, the more that child needs your positive influence in his or her life. And never, never forget how important being a teacher is. The very foundation of our modern world depends on teachers, as does the future success of each and every individual student.

Talent is not inherited—it is encouraged.

Effective Prevention Strategies 4

Prevention strategies are meant to instill in students a personal desire to behave in the classroom. They are also meant to create a positive atmosphere in the classroom that will be conducive to both teaching and learning.

Although little time needs to be spent employing prevention strategies, it is beneficial to detail a plan of methods you will use and to commit yourself to using them (Bosch, 2006). For positive, upbeat, and enthusiastic teachers, this will be easy. For the rest, it is a little tougher.

It is tougher if the teacher is

- Used to handling things as they come up
- Personally uncomfortable with displaying extroverted behaviors
- Convinced that time is not available to carry out the prevention strategies
- Comfortable with the way things are and sees no reason to change

These all are powerful reasons. I know that change is tough and that only those with a strong personal desire will change.

Please keep in mind as you go through the prevention strategies that some will appeal to you and others will not and that there may be some you may already use. Those that appeal to you should be noted in your personal Smart Discipline Plan at the end of this book.

Each of the prevention methods is simple. However, each has the potential of encouraging students to do the following:

- Cooperate with you and other teachers
- Have a desire to learn and be guided by you

Strategy: Welcome Students

Examples:

1. Welcome students at the door with either a verbal greeting or a handshake.

2. Tell a few students each day, "I'm glad you're here."

3. Greet a few students each day by putting a hand on their shoulders and saying something like, "Jim, how are you today?"

> **Note:** This simple idea produces radical results. Admittedly, it takes some time, but the payoff for the effort is large. Students will get the idea from your welcoming them that you care about them personally. This knowledge fosters a desire to cooperate.

One note of caution about touching, some students may pull away. However, the risk can be well worthwhile. A pat on the shoulder can establish a link between a teacher and student that will have a powerful and positive impact on the student.

Strategy: Express Appreciation

Instructions: First, check off from the list on page 29 the behaviors and qualities that are the most important to you to have students display.

Next, on a note card, list up to 10 behaviors and characteristics that you assign the highest priority. Place this card where you will automatically see it on a daily basis.

Then, say to a few students each day things such as,

- "Good job on staying in your seat today. . . . I appreciate it."
- "Thank you for being honest with me today."
- "I appreciated it when you came back to class right on time."
- "I'm proud of you for being persistent with getting your assignment done."
- "Thank you for being so cooperative today. . . . You made my day go better."
- "I noticed how hard you worked on getting along with your classmates today; thank you."

> **Note:** When you make these comments, be sure to say them to the student either in private or in a low voice. Except for a few students with exceptional self-esteem, most tend to get embarrassed when singled out for exemplary behavior. In fear of being labeled a nerd or teacher's pet, many students will even extinguish positive behaviors likely to single them out for public attention.

_____ Follows directions   _____ Enthusiastic

_____ Positive attitude   _____ Respectful

_____ Honesty   _____ Prompt

_____ Self-confidence   _____ Completes work

_____ Good manners   _____ Organized

_____ Good listener   _____ Attentive

_____ Friendly   _____ Sharing

_____ Trustworthy   _____ Volunteers

_____ Displays initiative   _____ Polite

_____ Sincere   _____ Cheerful

_____ Considerate   _____ Loyal

_____ Sense of humor   _____ Persistent

_____ Ambitious   _____ Goal-oriented

_____ Creative   _____ Kind

_____ Self-reliant   _____ Understanding

_____ Dependable   _____ Hard worker

_____ Calm   _____ Cooperative

_____ Determined   _____ Good memory

_____ Other: _____   _____ Other: _____

However, all students thrive on appreciation and positive feedback given in private. Such experiences not only foster future cooperation but self-esteem, as well. Positive feedback especially helps a student foster a belief that he or she has what it takes to succeed in school.

For optimum effect, keep your feedback short and sweet, and couple it with some evidence of the behavior or characteristic on which you are focusing. And do not pay any attention if a student rejects your positive comments. Secretly, these students greatly appreciate these comments, and their negative response is a cover-up for embarrassment.

If you encounter a negative response, do not try to force your point. Simply say, "I just wanted you to know," and walk away with a smile.

Strategy: Write a Note

Instructions: Use the same examples from the last segment on appreciation, and convey them in a note to the student. Be sure to do as follows:

- Keep it simple
- Keep it short
- Base it on behavior you have observed
- Say "thank you" in some fashion

Strategy: Write a Letter

Instructions: Same as above, but address it to the student's parents. Set a goal to send one letter home per week. Ask the school to spring for the postage.

Example:

> Dear Mr. and Mrs. Thompson:
>
> I thought you would like to know how cooperative James has been in my class. Today, I especially appreciated how well he followed directions and completed his work.
>
> Let me know if I can ever answer any questions for you about James's school work.
>
> Sincerely,
> Ms. Cindy Preston

> *Note:* The biggest objection to this is that it takes time. But it takes less time than you might think. If you use basically the same letter and keep it short, this should take less than five minutes per week.

You can do yourself a major favor by making sure that you send these letters home first to the parents of the students you are having the most difficulty with. This will not only help encourage positive behavior but also will likely enlist the parents as allies as well. This way, if you do have to call home later to discuss a problem, you will most likely get a much more positive response.

To save time, do your letters on a computer so you do not have to rewrite them each time.

For future reference, you may want to keep copies.

What an impact these letters will make! I can just see all the smiles, feel all the warm feelings, and predict all the resulting good behavior already.

Would you have liked more praise when you were a child? Could your students use some more too?

Strategy: Call Home

Instructions: Instead of writing a positive note to the parents, call them. Stick to the same rules as described with sending a note, but add one thing: smile when you are talking on the phone. They will not be able to see it, but they will be able to sense your enthusiasm.

Remember to keep the conversation focused on the positives. If negatives come up, explain that the purpose of your call was to express your appreciation and that you would be happy to call another time to help solve any difficulties. For the most part, you will not have to worry about this happening because most parents will be so thrilled with your positive call that they will not bring up problems. Be sure to keep a phone log to record information learned in these calls.

Strategy: Ask Personal Questions

Instructions: Start asking different students questions that will help you get to know them personally. For example,

- "Do you have a pet?" If so, ask what kind; if not, ask, "What kind would you like to have if you could have one?"
- "How do you get to school?" and "How long does it take?"
- "What's your favorite color?"
- "Who is your best friend?"
- "What's your favorite sport or hobby?"

Do not expect to keep the answers in memory. Write them down in a notebook later so you can refer to them and follow up with comments such as,

- "How's your dog Pete doing?"
- "Did you get wet walking to school today, or were you able to get a ride?"
- "I see you're wearing your favorite color today."
- "What have you and your friend Sue been up to lately?"
- "Have you been in any good volleyball games lately?"

> *Note:* Taking a personal interest in students' lives motivates students to take an interest in learning from and cooperating with the teacher. Also, a student who has experienced a teacher's personal interest is more likely to accept correction from that teacher.

Strategy: Transpose Critical Comments

Instructions: Review the sample destructive criticisms and their alternatives on page 33. Then fill out the blanks under "Your turn."

> *Note:* It is tough to stop using criticism. Using criticism to shape behavior is habitual in our culture. Changing to a positive approach takes some forethought, planning, and practice. Every bit of effort you put into it is well worthwhile because criticism is guaranteed to destroy a teacher-student relationship and spawn a desire for revenge.

As you seek a more positive approach, keep in mind that you will most likely slip up from time to time and criticize. Do not beat yourself up over it, but rather decide how you will handle the situation next time.

Remember, though, never to criticize a student in front of other students. To do so is to drop an H-bomb on any hopes you have of gaining this child's cooperation.

Destructive Criticisms and Sample Alternatives:

Criticism	Sample Alternative
You're lazy.	You're a hard worker and I expect you to act that way.
You're a liar.	You are an honest child, and I expect you to tell me the truth.
All you ever do is complain.	I handle complaints by appointment only. Would you like to make an appointment?
You're just plain mean. If I catch you hitting again, you'll be sorry.	Hitting is not allowed. I have made an appointment for you to talk to me about it at 3:15.
You've got the worst manners of anyone I know.	Earlier today I saw you using good manners. Would you consider using your good manners right now? Thank you.
Your attitude stinks. In fact, with an attitude like that, you will never amount to anything.	You seem like you're in a bad mood right now. It's not always easy to be positive, but a good attitude goes a long way with me.

Your turn: _____

_____

_____

_____

Strategy: Point Out Talents

Instructions: Pay attention to the strengths that individual students have and point them out to a few students each day.

Examples:

- "Trisha, you have a good sense of organization. I like the way you organized your thoughts in the report on the Civil War."
- "Bill, one of your talents seems to be in math. Last week you got a B on your final exam. You're getting better all the time."

- "Lynn, I heard from Ms. Brooks that you are one of her best music students. She thinks you have a natural talent for music."
- "Good speech, John. It was concise and to the point. Seems like you're a natural when it comes to speaking."

When you point out the evidence that a student has a specific talent, wonderful things happen. The student becomes motivated to work harder to develop that talent and builds a belief that says, "I have what it takes to be successful in school." And, of course, anyone who helps that student feel this way will gain the student's cooperation.

Choose your words carefully. Children take them for being true and construct beliefs out of them.

Note: This strategy allows a teacher to let students know in a nonthreatening way what behaviors are not allowed. It also allows students to know they are not "bad" for their actions but simply need to postpone the behavior until later.

Please remember that giving positive reinforcement should, if possible, be done in private. Private comments are taken to heart and have a powerful impact without getting the child labeled as teacher's pet.

Strategy: Predict Success

Instructions: These are the same as in the Point Out Talents strategy, plus a prediction of success is added.

Note: Do not worry if the student shrugs off your comments. You can count on a good share of the students taking your predictions to heart and living up to them.

Examples:

- "Trisha, with your talent for organization, you'll go far. I wouldn't be surprised if you become a successful business manager one day."
- "Bill, you continue to improve in math. You know, you could be a math teacher!"
- "Lynn, with your talent for music, I bet you could have a successful career using your musical talents one day."
- "John, someday you're going to speak in front of large groups and get paid lots of money for it."

Choose your words carefully. Children take them as being true and construct beliefs out of them.

Strategy: Make Appointments

Instructions: Whenever a student has a complaint or wants to argue a point, make an appointment to discuss the matter at a time you can speak in private. At the appointment, ask the student to explain his or her point of view. Clarify the child's perception, empathize with it, and state your decision. Keep the appointment under five minutes in length.

Example:

Student: Ms. Brooks, you treated me unfairly. Why did you take five points off for listing my textbook as a reference?

Teacher: John, that sounds like a complaint. I would like to give your complaint serious consideration, so let's make an appointment to talk about it. I have an opening at 12:45 or 3:00. Which would be better for you?

Student: I don't want any appointment. I want to know now!

Teacher: (smiling) I understand you would like to discuss it now, but I handle all legitimate complaints by appointment. Would 12:45 be okay, or would 3:00 be better?

Student: 12:45, I suppose, will be okay.

Teacher: I'm glad you came in, John. I appreciate your willingness to put off talking about your complaint until we could sit down together. Tell me what the problem is.

Student: The problem is that you took off five points for using my textbook as one of my three references for my report. That's not fair 'cause you never said we couldn't do that.

Teacher: Let me see if I understand you. You're upset because I docked you for using your text as a reference, and you think this is unfair because you didn't hear me say this wasn't allowed. Is that right?

Student: Yeah, that's it, and I want my five points back.

Teacher: I can see that those five points are very important to you. And you are right that it would be unfair for me to take off the points without warning. Unfortunately, John, I did tell the class about this. I'm sorry you didn't hear me. Because I did mention it, John, I won't be able to give your points back.

Student: But that's not fair!

Teacher: Yes, I understand you don't feel I'm being fair. However, I want you to know I really mean it when I say I appreciate your willingness to sit down and talk with me about it. Thank you. [Teacher, if comfortable with it, shakes hands with the student or pats the student on the back.]

There are some major advantages to using the appointment strategy. They include the following:

- Prevents power struggles
- Provides cooldown period
- Avoids embarrassment for teacher and student

- Gives teacher time to think out responses
- Gives students message that their issues will be taken seriously
- Reduces the number of frivolous complaints because only students serious about their point will tend to go to the trouble of coming in for an appointment

By predicting a student's success, you help create a self-fulfilling prophecy. As a bonus, encouragement fosters cooperation.

Strategy: Elicit Third-Party Encouragement

Instructions: Ask other teachers to observe your students around school and to report any good behavior to you. As you receive the reports, pass along what you heard to the individual students in private.

Examples:

- "Jerry, Ms. Kramer mentioned to me how you talked Jimmy out of fighting on the playground. Good job!"

- "Mr. Powers pulled me aside this morning in the staff meeting and told me about how you helped him clean up the mess in the hallway yesterday after school. Keep up the good work!"
- "Shelly, Ms. Perkins sure had some good things to say about you today. I'm proud of you for being such a positive student."

> **Note:** Please keep in mind that in our society, 99 percent of the positive feedback goes to well-behaved kids with positive attitudes. Certainly, they should continue to get their share of attention, but it is the "problem children" we need to turn around. Therefore, it behooves us to make a concerted effort to bring loads of positive feedback their way. Every bit we can funnel their way increases their chances for success in school and their desire to behave appropriately.

Strategy: List Misplaced Behaviors

Instructions: Tell the class that a misplaced behavior is a behavior that is perfectly appropriate somewhere else but not in the class. Brainstorm with the class what some of these behaviors are and list them on the blackboard.

Your list should end up looking something like this:

1. Running
2. Yelling
3. Interrupting
4. Talking out of turn
5. Engaging in horseplay
6. Chewing gum
7. Sleeping
8. Wrestling
9. Passing notes
10. Walking around
11. Talking to a friend
12. Teasing

Once the list is made, explain to the class that these are not "bad" behaviors but are rather "misplaced" and are not allowed at school. Later, you can refer back to misplaced behaviors as needed.

Examples:

- "Cindy, talking in class is one of those misplaced behaviors. Can you save it for later?"
- "Craig, running out of class is one of those misplaced behaviors. Can you save it for after school? Thanks."

The Smart Discipline System 5

In this chapter, I present all that you need to know to use my Smart Discipline System. This system is used by both teachers and parents in the United States and in other countries around the world.

I think its popularity is due to the ease and effectiveness of use. The whole purpose of the system is to lead students down a path where they end up choosing to stop *themselves* from misbehaving.

Research data shows that when the Smart Discipline System is used schoolwide, there is an approximately 75 percent decrease in school suspensions and discipline referrals to the office. Best of all, teachers report major reductions in classroom misbehavior, making more time available for teaching (Koenig, 2006).

The Smart Discipline System is especially suited for a school that is seeking a discipline or classroom management plan that can be used by all of the teachers. When you think about it, it makes a lot of sense to have all the teachers at a school on the same page. We all know that consistency with students is a basic tenet of success, yet the predominant mode of operation in schools is to leave discipline up to a myriad of discipline approaches as varied as the number of teachers on staff. What works best for teachers, students, and parents alike is a consistent approach.

As validation through research is so important these days, I have included questionnaires for administrators, teachers, and counselors in the Note From the Author on page 101. You can copy these and use them to collect the data to document the effectiveness of the Smart Discipline System and Smart Charts at your school.

In the previous chapter, I offered a smorgasbord of prevention strategies designed to get even the most challenging of students to want to cooperate with you. Used together with the Smart Discipline System, you will find that you will be able to manage your classroom with ease and delight.

Strategy: The Smart Discipline System

Instructions: The Smart Discipline System revolves around the use of my Smart Charts. Following are the directions to set up and use the charts. While the initial effort in doing so may take some time, in both the long and short run you will find that you will save tremendous amounts of time by using the system.

1. Using the list of misbehaviors in Chapter 1 and your list of misplaced behaviors, develop a list of up to seven rules. Most likely you will develop these in concert with the rest of the teachers. They will likely vary from grade level to grade level. However, the same rules should apply in classrooms at the same grade level. A list of sample rules appears on pages 41 to 42. Please note: Rules should be written in language easily grasped by your students.

2. Develop a list of five privileges and/or consequences that are within your control. A list of sample privileges appears on page 42. Please note: Reduce to one or two words; words that are short enough to list in a box on the Smart Charts and again, easy to understand.

3. Rank the five privileges and/or consequences from one to five with the least important privilege being number one and the most important number five.

4. Place the rules and the privileges on the Smart Charts (see Smart Chart on page 46.) The privileges should be written on the lines lettered D through H.

5. Copy and distribute the Smart Charts to your students. I suggest that at least once per week, usually on Monday, the students are asked to write out the class rules on the charts; the idea is to help teach and reinforce the classroom rules. On the rest of the charts that you distribute each day, you may want to have the rules preprinted.

6. Explain the Smart Charts to your students. Tell them:
   a. From now on every day you will ask them to take out their Smart Chart, and you will have them put the date and privileges in the boxes of the charts. Every Monday you will have them copy the classroom rules on their charts.
   b. They will be required to carry their Smart Charts with them to classes and activities outside of the classroom as well. For example, to music, art, and physical education.
   c. You will explain how the Smart Charts work but would like them to first fill in one of the Monday charts with the rules and privileges.
   d. If they break a rule, you or any other teacher in the school will ask them to take out their Smart Charts and you will put the number of the rule they broke in the box lettered "A."
   e. If they break another rule or the same rule again, another box will be filled in with the number of the rule(s) that were broken. For each rule broken, another box will be filled in.

    f. The first three boxes are free squares. Basically they are warnings that rules have been broken and if misbehavior continues, privileges will be lost or consequences imposed.

    g. When boxes that have privileges or consequences in them are filled in, they will lose the privilege for the rest of the day or suffer the consequences listed in those boxes.

    h. Every day they will be required to take their Smart Charts home to be signed by their parents and returned the next day. For any day that the Smart Charts are not brought back signed, an infraction will be listed in the first square of their charts.

7. When infractions of the rules take place, go back to the student's desk and ask the student to hand you his or her Smart Chart. Quietly ask the student what rule he or she violated (Please note: Do not get into a discussion. If the student is contentious, say, "I don't have time to discuss this right now. We can talk about this later if you wish"). Note the number of the rule that was violated in the next available box and go back to teaching.

8. On Mondays, have each child copy the rules and consequences on their "Monday" charts. (Please note: Younger children who are unable to write will need to have assistance in writing in the rules and consequences.) Every other day have them date their charts and fill in the consequences. While they are doing this, walk through the class and spot check to see if the previous days charts were signed be the parents. If not, mark an infraction. Also, check the charts for notes from parents.

9. Make sure to take away privileges or impose consequences the same day of the rule infractions.

10. Make an effort to point out positive behavior and make note of it on the charts. Especially do this with students who have behavior problems.

Sample Rules:

(Please note: The first two rules are strongly recommended)

1. Smart Charts must be signed by parents each day and kept available at all times at school.

2. School and homework must be done properly and handed in on time.

3. Speak to teachers and fellow students with respect.

4. Remain awake and attentive at all times.

5. Raise your hand for permission to speak.

6. Ask for permission before leaving your seat.

7. Resolve disagreements without hitting.

8. Respect the property of others.

9. Be on time.

10. Do not cheat.

Sample Privileges and Consequences:

1. Exclusion from recess

2. Time-out in another classroom

3. Isolated lunch

4. Detention

5. Extra homework

6. Essay on what rules were broken, why they were broken, and other possible choices of behavior and/or responses the next time

7. Move to desk closest to the teacher

8. Conference with teacher

9. Conference with teacher and principal

10. Call home to parents

Guidelines:

1. When a rule is violated, mark the number of the rule that was violated in the first box. I recommend using a red ink pen or Sharpie to mark infractions on the Smart Charts. Continue on marking boxes in alphabetical order as rules are violated. If you are a specialty teacher, also sign your name in the box or identify what class the child was in when the rule was violated.

2. Do not give warnings or second chances. In other words, do not say things like, "If you don't quit it, I'm going to put an infraction on your chart." Instead just go ahead and do it. This will teach your students you mean business the first time—without having to raise your voice.

3. When taking away privileges or imposing a consequence, express empathy and belief they will do better next time. For example, "This is really a bummer for you to miss recess today. But I'm sure you will do better tomorrow."

4. If you do not know which student broke the rule, give everyone you think may have been involved an infraction.

5. If behavior is exhibited that is dangerous to other students or to you, report it immediately to the school office.

Frequently Asked Questions:

Question: What if a student continually does not bring his or her Smart Charts back with a parent's signature?

Answer: If a parent repeatedly fails to sign the daily Smart Charts, then the teacher or counselor can call home to make sure the parents know what to do. If the problem persists, then a parent, teacher, or administrator conference is scheduled to solve the issue. If the problem still persists, then simply start the child's chart each day with the red number in the first box. The number corresponds with the rule about having your Smart Chart available and prepared at all times. It could be a legitimate issue, but I have not had that problem in the schools that use Smart Charts yet. Most parents, even the control freaks, tend to comply before their child will be held responsible for his or her parent's inaction.

Question: What if a student gets really upset when I put an infraction on his or her chart?

Answer: Speak quietly and softly. Tell the student that you will speak with him or her later if he or she wishes. Move away and go back to teaching.

Question: Won't implementing the Smart Charts take a lot of my teaching time?

Answer: It should take less than five minutes a day to check the charts and have the students fill in their rules and consequences. As just a few students on any given day are likely to misbehave, it should just take a few moments to note the infractions on their charts. In the long run, the Smart Charts dramatically reduce misbehavior. The result will be MORE teaching time, not less.

Question: Why should I do this with all of my students when most of them don't misbehave? Isn't it a waste of time to have Smart Charts for well-behaved students?

Answer: One of the good things about the Smart Charts is that they keep well-behaved students motivated to stay well behaved. This is because students learn vicariously. When they see other students being reprimanded for their misbehavior, it further reinforces their decision to not break classroom rules. Additionally, the charts have a space for positive comments that can be used to make note of their good behavior.

Question: How will I know who lost what privileges?

Answer: Usually, this is not a problem, for on any given day only one or two students in a class are likely to misbehave enough to lose privileges, so it will be easy to remember. Still, keeping in mind that teachers have a lot to keep track of, we have designed a Master Smart Chart (see page 47) that can be laminated. With this organizer, you can list student's names and mark infractions on it as you give them out. This is a quick and nifty way of keeping track.

Question: Won't it be embarrassing for a student to have me walk over, ask them to get out their Smart Charts, and mark an infraction?

Answer: Here are two things to keep in mind. First, think in terms of getting a traffic ticket. Is it embarrassing standing on the side of the road with the police car's lights flashing? You bet it is! And, it is part of the consequence for breaking the rules. Now please do not misunderstand. I am NOT saying to use the Smart Charts to ridicule students or to make them feel bad in any way. Quite to the contrary, I ask teachers to quietly and respectfully go about the task of marking infractions on the Smart Charts. If a student still feels embarrassed about this, I hope this negative feeling would turn into a positive motivator of future good behavior.

Question: Why does every student need a Smart Chart Book? Why not just have the teachers keep a list on their desks?

Answer: For two reasons: First, one of the major tasks of the Smart Charts is to teach students that they are in control of their own behavior and to motivate them to use that control to comply with the rules. Having the individual charts seems to create this sense of control for students. Second, the individual Smart Charts have to be taken home each day to be signed by the parents. This creates the double-edged-sword effect where a child has to answer for his or her behavior at home and at school.

Question: What about ADD and ADHD students? They have so much energy that needs to be burned up. Wouldn't it be a negative to take away their recess?

Answer: This certainly can be a legitimate concern. In such a case I would suggest modifying their recess time to include walking laps; anything that would burn up energy but would exclude them from being able to join in with group activities.

Advantages to Using the Smart Charts:

1. *Is Research Based.* Schools using the Smart Charts report major reductions in misbehavior. Principals report referrals to the office for discipline drop by 75 percent or more and suspensions drop by over 80 percent. Teachers report increased teaching time; significantly less time spent on discipline; and quiet, orderly classrooms and hallways (Koenig, 2006).

2. *Closes Communication Gap Between School and Home.* Much like in earlier generations, if students get in trouble at school they also get in trouble at home. And, the feedback to the parents is daily—letting students know that not only will they have to pay the consequences at school but their parents will find out right away if they misbehave.

3. *Creates Consistency.* One of the things we all know is that to be effective with children you have to be consistent. Yet every teacher has his or her own style of disciplining. The Smart Charts put all the teachers on the same page with discipline—the result being a consistent and effective approach with the students.

4. *Is Easy to Use.* Teachers will not use what takes too much time or what is too complicated. The Smart Charts take little time, are easy to use, and produce immediate and consistent results.

5. *Self-Motivates Students.* Teachers usually wait until a student misbehaves and then figures out what action to take. This approach is often ineffective in curbing misbehavior. The Smart Charts, on the other hand, let students know what the rules are along with the consequences they will face for violating the rules. Plus, they know there is a system for keeping track of violations and for enforcement of consequences. The effect in the long run is a system that motivates students to behave at school.

6. *Helps New Teachers.* Many first year teachers express great trepidation over how to handle discipline and a number of these fail miserably at the task. It is estimated that over 30 percent of teachers quit teaching within five years of starting because of discipline issues. The Smart Charts give them an easy and effective way to handle discipline.

7. *Benefits All Socioeconomic Levels.* Even schools where parental involvement, education, and family incomes are low report dramatic reductions of misbehavior with the use of the Smart Charts.

8. *Assists Substitute Teachers.* When substitute teachers walk into a classroom, misbehavior typically escalates. We think this is because the threat of consequences disappears. The Smart Charts are easy to teach to substitute teachers, giving them an effective means of behavior control.

9. *Improves the Learning Environment.* The end goal of the Smart Charts is to improve student academic performance—the thought being that for students to learn, it is necessary to provide them with a calm orderly learning environment. While we have established that use of the Smart Charts helps create this kind of environment, we have not yet established a link to improved academic scores. This is our next task.

Rule violations should be tied to specific consequences.

SMART CHART

_____   _____

Student's Name   **Today's Date**

Classroom/School Rules

1. _____

2. _____

3. _____

4. _____

5. _____

6. _____

7. _____

_____ A	_____ B	_____ C	_____ D
_____ E	_____ F	_____ G	_____ H

Note to Parents: Please sign this form and date below. Your child should turn it in tomorrow or the next school day. Numbers written on the chart by the teacher correspond to the number of the rule that was broken.

_____   _____

Parent/Guardian Signature   **Date**

Comments:

_____

_____

_____

_____

MASTER SMART CHART

Student Name	A	B	C	D	E	F	G	H

Strategies for Minor Misbehaviors (Plan A)

6

Plan A strategies are designed to work on common disruptive behaviors that any student might exhibit. They could range from pencil tapping to whispering to throwing things and so on.

Also, Plan A methods, although quick and easy to use, should produce immediate results. By just using one or two of them, the misbehaving student should stop the offensive behavior right away and redirect his or her attention to the learning task at hand. More important, little if any time needs to be taken away from teaching to employ these techniques.

As you review these strategies, keep in mind that some will work wonders with some students but work not at all with others. Do not be distressed by this; just try something else until you find what works with that child. Also, remember that some of these techniques will fit your teaching style and personality better than others. List the ones that you like in your personal Smart Discipline Plan under "Plan A Strategies" on page 95.

Strategy: Use Friendly Evil Eye

Instructions: Make eye contact with the misbehaving student, smile, and shake head slightly.

Note: Keep this nonthreatening by smiling. Do not let it interrupt your teaching.

Strategy: Invade Space

Instructions: Keep teaching while you walk over and stand by the offending student. Do not bother to make eye contact, but smile and continue teaching.

Note: A majority of students will stop misbehaving just so you will vacate their space.

Strategy: Touch Shoulder

Instructions: While invading space as above, rest your hand on the student's shoulder as you continue to smile and teach.

Note: The smile and the touch give a powerful nonverbal message that you care about the student and are asking in a friendly way for the wrongful behavior to be ceased.

Beware of the students who react adversely to touch. If a student pulls away and says something like, "Leave me alone. I didn't do anything!" simply whisper, "We'll talk about it later," and move away from the student.

Strategy: Whisper Technique

Instructions: Walk close enough to the student to whisper something like, "Cindy, would you please spit out your gum?" Do not wait for a response. Assume the answer is "yes" by quickly saying, "Thank you," breaking eye contact, and moving away.

Note: The Whisper Technique conveys to the student the following messages:

1. You are not afraid.
2. You care about the student.
3. You do not want to embarrass anyone.
4. You accept the student but not the behavior.
5. You do not want to get into an argument.
6. You trust the student to willingly comply.

By breaking eye contact and moving away quickly, you short-circuit possible power struggles. Maintaining eye contact and staying in the student's space gives the message that you do not trust the student to comply and are there to force him or her to do so. The opposite message is given when you whisper your request, break eye contact, and move away. This strategy will most likely achieve willing compliance.

Strategy: Smile and Request

Instructions: Either by whispering or by speaking to the student in private, ask the student if he or she would consider changing the behavior. Say, "Thank you," and vacate the student's space.

> **Note:** Most of us will respond positively to someone who smiles at us and asks us to consider doing something. It works like a charm, especially when compared with telling us to do something.

Examples:

- "Greg, would you consider not drumming your fingers on your desk? Thank you."
- "Mandy, would you consider taking off that head visor? Thank you."

When seeking a change in behavior from a strong-willed child, the Smile and Request strategy is a must. With these kids and those with oppositional disorders, commands will result in power struggles nearly every time. However, a smiling request most often will result in a positive response.

Strategy: Allow Thinking Time

Instructions: When a student makes a request that you will most likely deny, respond instead with, "Let me think about it. I'll let you know later."

> **Note:** Employing this strategy has two major advantages.
>
> 1. You do not have to stop teaching.
> 2. You avoid arguments and power struggles.

It also does, in fact, give you some time to consider the request and your response. This is good because if sometimes a quick "no" later turns to a "yes," it teaches a child to keep arguing until the child gets his or her way.

Plus, given time to think, you may come up with an alternative response satisfactory to both parties. One other benefit is that students tend to be "good as gold" while you are considering their requests.

For this to work as an ongoing strategy, occasionally, you will have to grant permission. To make sure this happens, you can also respond with "Let me think about it" to some requests you are sure to grant.

Strategy: Change Locations

Instructions: Purposely leave a desk open near the front of the room but still in line with the other desks. When a student misbehaves, whisper to him, "Brad, would you mind sitting over here? Thank you." Move away and go on teaching.

If the student does not comply, go back over and whisper, "Brad, did I ask you in a polite way? Good. Thank you for cooperating." If still noncompliant, say, "Brad, I see you didn't move. We'll talk about it later." Smile, move away, and go back to teaching.

> **Note:** Most students will comply right away. When they move, their behavior will change, at least for a while. Changing locations causes a child to stop doing what he or she is doing in order to get oriented to the new location.

If a student refuses to comply, withdraw and let yourself and the student out of the power struggle. Make an appointment to discuss the situation later. Trying to force the issue is a real loser for everyone involved because power struggles distress the whole class and can even end up in violence.

Later, when you can speak to the student alone, discuss what happened. Be sure to indicate future consequences for noncompliant behavior.

Strategy: Exercise the Quiet Signal

Instructions: Explain to the class that when you want the whole class to be in their seats and completely quiet, you will raise your hand. Explain that when they see your hand go up, everyone is to return to their seats, raise their hands, and keep them up until everyone is seated and quiet with their hands up.

Strategy: State Your Want

Instructions: Once you have the class quiet and paying attention, state what you need for them to do.

> **Note:** Clear and concise statements of needs can often get a class back on track after involvement in highly participatory (and noisy) activities. A very nice pattern of expectancy can be set up by using this strategy with the Quiet Signal. In other words, if you start using the Quiet Signal and always follow it with a statement of what you want, students will quickly get used to your calm and in-charge approach.

Examples:

- "What I want right now is for everyone to work quietly on his or her assignment."
- "What I need right now is for everyone to listen to my instructions."

> **Note:** Elementary-grade students enthusiastically respond to this method. It saves on your voice, too!

Strategy: Give Information

Instructions: Point out what you are observing at the moment. Simply report the information to the student and do not give instructions.

Examples:
- "Dawn, you were five minutes late this morning."
- "John, I didn't get your makeup work."
- "Kerry, you were running in the hall."

Strategy: Convey Qualities Plus Expectations

Instructions: When a student misbehaves, label the child with a positive quality and tell the child you expect him or her to act that quality out in a certain way.

> **Note:** Being labeled with a positive attribute startles students. It is something rarely done. Maybe this is why it works so well. Besides gaining compliance, this strategy also builds self-esteem while strengthening the teacher-student relationship. I highly recommend using it liberally.

Examples:

- "Ann, you are an honest person. I expect you to be truthful."
- "Clint, you have good manners. I expect you to be polite."
- "Katie, you are a cooperative person, and I need you to cooperate with me right now."

Do not make the mistake many teachers make. That is, they stop themselves from using this technique. If the student's behavior does not always measure up, some teachers feel that focusing on that quality would be a lie. Others feel that telling a student he or she has a certain quality will cause the child to think the child does not need to improve.

In response, I will point out that every child possesses both the positive and negative of every quality. The quality they end up believing themselves to possess is mainly determined from feedback from others. Therefore, adults can greatly assist children in adopting positive qualities by assigning the quality to the child as if it were fact.

Label a person with a positive attribute, and you give that person something to live up to. For many, you can help create a self-fulfilling prophecy.

Strategy: Give Choices

Instructions: For strong-willed children, this method is especially effective. The children need a sense of control, so you give it to them by giving them choices.

Examples:

- "Brian, would you rather go back to your seat and do your work there, or would you rather do it at the empty desk over here?"
- "Lucinda, would you rather cooperate with me right now and be able to go out for recess, or would you rather sit in the principal's office during recess?"
- "Bonnie, would you rather apologize to Bruce now or make an appointment to talk with me about it during lunch time?"

> **Note:** If the student either does not respond or says, "I don't know," simply say, "Sounds like we need to talk about it later; let's make an appointment for 3:05."

For the most effective use of this strategy, remember to smile and be friendly. Your positive energy will produce positive results.

Strategy: Respect the Struggle

Instructions: With this strategy, you show empathy for how difficult it is to control certain behaviors and request future cooperation.

> **Note:** When individuals perceive that someone understands their struggles, they feel appreciated. When they feel appreciated, they will likely cooperate. The trick is making sure your empathy is real. Students have an uncanny ability to discern whether or not someone is being sincere. If you are sincere, your students will know it and will respond with cooperation.

Examples:

- "Jennifer, I understand that it is difficult to control your temper when you get teased. May I count on you to control your temper for the rest of the day?"
- "Frank, I know how hard it is to concentrate when we just have a few hours left before Christmas vacation starts. Would you consider staying in your seat while we finish our math lesson? Thank you."

Strategy: Answer Questions With Questions

Instructions: Some students have unceasing questions. Some ask absurd questions. Others ask questions they already know the answer to or could find out the answer to with minimal effort.

A teacher can both save time and teach self-reliance by answering questions with questions as in the examples below.

> **Note:** Consistent use of Answering Questions With Questions will give the whole class the message that you expect them to be self-reliant. However, make sure you shoot your questions back in a friendly manner.

Examples:

Student: (for the third time) When are we going to start our party?

Teacher: What time do you think?

Student: How do you spell *achieve?*

Teacher: How could you find out?

Student: Do I have to type my report?

Teacher: What do you suppose?

Inherent in this strategy is the danger of coming across as a sarcastic or uncaring person. This would be counterproductive. To guard against this, when the student answers your question appropriately, respond with a smile, a pat on the shoulder, and a kind word.

For those few students who keep coming back with questions (probably for the attention), when you run either out of patience or out of time, ask the student, "Would you consider not asking me any more questions for today?" If you can carry this out while being nice about it, you will be surprised with the results.

An added touch is to tell the student as he or she is leaving for the day that you appreciated him or her cooperating with you. This way, the student goes home feeling good and comes back the next day eager to cooperate with you again.

Respect the struggle by explaining, "Anything worth doing is worth doing poorly, until we practice enough to do it well."

Strategy: Do Research

Instructions: For the next two weeks, ask other teachers the question, "What works best for you to deal with _____?" Fill in the blank with one of the behaviors you listed in Chapter 1 on page 2. Take the strategies that appeal to you, and list them in your personal Smart Discipline Plan.

Please note: Review the Plan A strategies that appeal to you and make note of them on your personal Smart Discipline Plan on page 95.

> **Note:** Over the years, teachers come up with their own "bags of tricks" to gain cooperation in the classroom. Typically, the methods that teachers continually use are the ones that consistently get immediate results and are quick and easy to use. Most teachers are more than willing to share what works for them. All you need to do is ask.

Strategies for the Most Difficult Misbehaviors (Plan B)

7

Plan B strategies are for use with a particular student who continuously acts out despite the use of prevention and Plan A strategies. Typically, these are the students who get labeled as problem students, troublemakers, defiant, ADHD, oppositional, or simply out of control.

These are the students who truly are at risk. If some way cannot be found to motivate them to adopt behaviors and beliefs conducive to learning, they will end up dropping out. In the meantime, they will spend most of their time disrupting the class (Mendler & Curwin, 1999).

Therefore, for the sake of the student, the teacher, and the rest of the class, an effective plan of discipline must motivate the student to

- Follow school rules
- Cooperate with the teacher
- Have a desire to learn

Simply controlling a student's behavior is not enough. Compliance, cooperation, and learning must result for a student to be successful in school (F. Jones, 2000).

As with the prevention and Plan A strategies, keep in mind that some Plan B strategies will fit your teaching and personality style better than others. Make a mental note of the ones that appeal to you and also record them in your personal Smart Discipline Plan on page 96.

Strategy: Write a Note

Instructions: Write a note to the student describing the problem. Request in the note what action you would like the student to take.

> *Note:* What do you expect students will do when they get notes like these? Most likely, they will comply. If they do not, there are no hard feelings or power struggles. You simply try something else.

Examples:

> Carmen, I have noticed lately that you have been out of your seat without permission. Would you please raise your hand and get permission before getting out of your seat?
>
> Thank you,
> Ms. Simpson

> Terry, this morning you wore your sunglasses in class. Would you consider not wearing them in my class?
>
> Thank you,
> Mr. Viator

> Bev, your makeup work hasn't been handed in. Would you please have it in by tomorrow?
>
> Thanks,
> Mr. Crawford

Strategy: Express Strong Feelings

Instructions: In private, completely out of sight and hearing of other students, strongly express your feelings and ask for what you want.

> *Note:* Do not justify your feelings or request. Keep it short and to the point. If the student tries to blame someone else, respond with, "Yes, I understand what you are saying; however, can I count on you to _____ ?"

Our love, trust, and admiration go to those who listen to us.

Examples:

- "Brittney, I got very angry when you shoved Cheryl in the hall. May I count on you to not shove other students?"
- "Jeremy, I get extremely frustrated when you keep getting out of your seat. Would you please stay in your seat the rest of the day?"
- "Chris, when you are disrespectful to me I see red. May I count on you to be polite with me?"

If the student wants to draw you into an argument, back out of it, saying, "Sounds like this needs to be discussed further. Let's talk about it at 3:00 this afternoon. Can you come then, or would tomorrow at 12:45 be better?"

Some will take you up on your offer to talk. Those who do could most likely benefit from either a mini-counseling session or a cooperative planning session. These are the next two strategies.

Strategy: Arrange Mini-Counseling Session

Instructions: Arrange to speak with the misbehaving student where you can sit face-to-face without a desk between you. Start off by saying something like, "Stephanie, usually when students aren't cooperating with me, they have a personal reason. Would you like to discuss your reason or would you rather keep it to yourself?"

If she opts to not talk about it, respond with, "It's okay to not talk about it. I just wanted you to know I'm here if you want to talk. In the meantime, may I count on your cooperation?"

If she does want to talk, ask open-ended questions and clarify feelings. Keep it to less than five minutes, and invite her to tell you if she would like to talk again.

If more than a couple of these sessions are needed or if significant problems are mentioned, consult with the school counselor about referring the student for help.

Note: Some kids act out in the classroom in reaction to what is going on in their personal lives. Just having someone who cares enough to listen can make a major difference in the student's life and classroom behavior.

Strategy: Schedule Cooperative Planning Session

Instructions: Make an appointment to meet in private with the student. Describe to the student how you see the problem. Ask for the student's thoughts on how it could be solved.

Examples:

Teacher: Jason, I'm glad you came in for your appointment. I want to talk about how after lunch you seem to not pay attention to me. It seems like you just stare off into space. What are your thoughts on how you could pay attention to me in the afternoons?

Student: I don't know.

Teacher: Would you like to hear how some other students handle that problem?

Student: If I have to.

Teacher: Well, some students come up and sit in my reserved desk. The change in location seems to help. After a while, they go back to their own desk. What do you think?

Student: Well, I don't like the idea much. There must be a better way.

Teacher: Okay, let's brainstorm together and write down all the possibilities. Then you can tell me which you like best.

Student: All right. How about my putting my head down for a while or maybe you could come by and let me know if I'm spaced out. Sometimes I don't even realize I'm doing it!

The intent of the cooperative planning session is to get the student focused on providing solutions. Occasionally, this approach works like magic. It is well worth trying.

> ***Note:*** The difference between the Cooperative Planning Session and the Mini-Counseling Session strategies is the intent. In the mini-counseling session, the focus is on getting the student to open up and talk about what is going on in his or her life. By talking, it is hoped that either the student will bond with the teacher and develop a desire to cooperate or will reveal information pertinent to the student's life that can be dealt with by the school counselor.

Strategy: Chart Behavior and Consequences

Instructions: Refer to the section titled "Establish Classroom Rules, Consequences and Rewards" on pages 86 to 87. Be sure to involve the parents by sending the charts home for their signature.

If the opportunity arises, you may also offer to supply the parents with Smart Charts for them to use at home with their own rules and consequences. Some parents may jump at the chance. When you think about it, the kids causing you trouble in class are probably also acting out at home. The parents may be grateful for some suggestions.

Strategy: Use Time-Out

Instructions: Decide on locations for time-out. These may include (a) a place in the classroom separate from view of the class, (b) a chair in an upper or lower grade level, or (c) a chair in the principal's office.

> ***Note:*** When sending a student to time-out, do not lecture or give work to be done. If using another teacher's room or the principal's office, ask these people not to get into a discussion with the student. Do not allow the student to take anything to time-out. However, inform the student that he or she can decide to come back when ready to cooperate with the rest of the class.

Whisper to the student, "Would you please move to the time-out area? Thank you." Move away and go back to teaching. If the student does not go, whisper, "Did I ask you politely? Good, please move to the time-out, then." If the child still does not go, say privately, "I see you decided not to go. That's okay. We'll talk about it later." Go back to teaching.

If the child does not go to time-out after a couple of requests, this may be a signal that you have a very angry or disturbed student on your hands. The worst thing you can do at this point is to try to force the child to do something.

To calm the situation down, you may well want to back off as in the example given above. Or you may want to communicate in a note.

With highly agitated and upset students, be sure to vacate their space and break eye contact. Your main goal is to stay safe by preventing a power struggle and allowing the student time to cool down. Once the student is calm, make an appointment to discuss what happened and future consequences for refusing to move to time-out.

Please note: Any violence or threats of violence should be reported immediately, as well as any talk of suicide.

Strategy: Change Volume and Tempo

Instructions: If a student raises his or her voice or is obviously angry and upset, lower your voice and slow your speech down.

If you speak slowly and softly, angry students most likely will follow suit. When they do, they calm down.

> *Note:* Anger is normally conveyed with a loud voice. The usual way to respond is with a louder voice. This escalates the anger.

Strategy: Encourage Student Involvement

Instructions: If a student is highly agitated and will not calm down, ask if he or she would be willing to go out in the hall for a while and talk it out with another student. Let the student pick the person, if possible.

Or, if you have a student who is apparently experiencing personal problems, refer the student to a peer counselor, if available. Also consider referrals to school-based support groups or anger management programs.

Other students can also be involved to help with withdrawn students. This can be accomplished by requesting that an outgoing student or group of students help by going out of their way to include the withdrawn student. This can make a powerful difference in a kid's life.

A time-out or cool-down period often gives you and the student time to think about the situation and regain composure.

Strategy: Build Relationships

Instructions: With your problem students, be sure to concentrate on building your relationships with them. To do so, review and enact some of the appropriate relationship-building methods described in Chapter 4. These included

1. Welcome students (see page 28)

2. Express appreciation (see page 28)

3. Write a note (see page 30)

4. Write a letter (see page 30)

5. Call home (see page 31)

6. Ask personal questions (see page 32)

7. Transpose critical comments (see page 32)

8. Point out talents (see page 33)

9. Predict success (see page 34)

10. Elicit third-party encouragement (see page 37)

> ***Note:*** Problem students usually draw huge amounts of negativity from authority figures. As they do so, relationships deteriorate, as does the student's desire to cooperate with the education process.

What a relief it is for a student with problems when you take the time and effort to build a positive relationship with him or her. Such a relief, in fact, that it can fuel the student with the encouragement necessary to turn his or her attitude and behavior around.

Strategy: Use Activities for Leverage

Instructions: If the misbehaving student participates in sports, band, cheerleading, or any other extracurricular activity, consult with the teacher in charge. Agree on classroom rules that must be followed for the student to participate in the activities on a given day.

> ***Note:*** For some students, activities are so important that they will do anything to participate, including cooperating with classroom rules.

In other words, if the student does not follow the rules on any certain day, the student does not participate in that day's practice or activity. The student starts over with a new chance the next day. Make sure you inform the parents of your plans and enlist their cooperation.

Follow-through is a must with this strategy. Sticking to disallowing participation can be tough when a big event is scheduled. If the student is allowed to participate regardless of rule violations, the student will learn that he or she can operate in the classroom with impunity.

Therefore, before employing this strategy, decide whether or not you (and the coach) are willing to "stick to your guns." If so, leveraging activities may be just the strategy you need to gain a student's positive cooperation.

Strategy: Analyze and Plan

Instructions: When perplexed about what to do next with a student after you have tried a number of strategies to no avail, it is time to analyze the problem and write out a plan of action. As you do so, answer these questions:

- What are the behaviors in need of change?
- What are the expected behaviors?
- What have I tried?
- What worked?
- What did not work?
- What are three strategies I could try next?

Note: You are welcome to photocopy the worksheet on pages 71 to 72. Sometimes, writing things out can help. Be sure to save your worksheets to refer to if conferences are needed.

Strategy: Inform Parents

Instructions: Call the student's parents and say to them, "I would like to tell you what behaviors I have been seeing in the classroom, so I can get your thoughts." Describe the behaviors and ask, "Can you suggest anything that might help encourage your child to cooperate at school?"

Note: Do not tell students you will be calling. Parents typically believe whomever they hear from first. And you can be sure if students know you will be calling, they will run home to explain their versions of how they have been treated so unfairly. If students do not know you are calling, you will not have to overcome this obstacle.

When speaking with the parents, stay away from labels and blame. Neither is productive.

Strategy: Give Responsibilities

Instructions: Use your creativity to come up with ways the problem student can assist you or others around school. Once decided on, ask the student, "Would you consider helping me with _____?"

> ***Note:*** Most students will say yes. When they say yes, they are at the same time agreeing to cooperate with you. Amazingly enough, this can establish a pattern of continued cooperation.

Strategy: Encourage Involvement

Instructions: Encourage problem students to get involved with organized school activities. Volunteer to help get them started, or get another student to help facilitate the process.

The payoff for getting a student to participate can be big. It has the potential of getting the student to see himself or herself in a more positive light. It may even instill a desire to come to school!

> ***Note:*** Remember that uncooperative students normally have low self-esteem and often believe, "I don't have what it takes to be successful in school." Because of their negative beliefs, few participate in extracurricular activities. Also, because of these same beliefs, they need someone behind them to encourage them.

Strategy: Plan for Amends

Instructions: If a student does something for which he or she needs to make amends, make an appointment to discuss the matter. Ask the student how he or she plans to make things right. If the student responds with, "I don't know," come back with, "Would you like me to tell you how other students make things right when they do the same thing you did?" List the alternatives and ask if the student has any other suggestions.

> ***Note:*** Too many students continually misbehave and have nothing happen. No consequences are faced or amends made. When this happens, it is too bad for the teacher and the student.

Once the alternatives are laid out, ask the student to pick one. Agree on when the student will do it and how you will know it was done.

It is too bad for the teacher because unchecked disruptive behavior escalates. It is too bad for the student because the student will eventually meet up with inescapable consequences. If his or her behavior has gotten way out of line, those consequences may ruin the student's life.

Lucky is the student who has a teacher who enforces consequences and insists amends be made, where appropriate.

Strategy: Deliver "I" Messages

Instructions: Design a three-part message to deliver to a student about his or her behavior. Plan it in advance, and deliver the message in private.

The three parts should include (1) a description of the problem behavior, (2) the feelings that the behavior stirs in you, and (3) the results of the behavior.

Examples:

1. "I noticed you passing notes."

2. "It irritates me when students don't pay attention in class."

3. "When I get irritated, it's tough for me to teach and I lose my patience."

Note: If the student says, "Who cares?" respond with, "I just wanted you to know." Avoid telling the student what to do about it. Not telling the student what to do prevents backlash and gives the message that the student is intelligent enough to figure out a plan of action.

Sometimes, parents do not have the foggiest idea of what is really going on at school. Direct communication with parents is often a must to solve problems.

Strategy: Assign Student Essay

Instructions: Give the problem student the assignment of writing an essay. In the essay, ask the student to answer the following questions:

- What was the problem in class today?
- How did you feel during and after the problem took place?
- What did you do about the problem?
- How did it work?
- What will you do next time the problem comes up?

> **Note:** This strategy has good potential for helping students develop insight into their behavior. It also can provide a constructive method for the students to explain their viewpoint. This can help students calm down and provide a release for their anger.

Ask the student to turn in the report the next school day. When handed in, make an appointment to discuss it.

As an added benefit, a student with a plan of how to handle a problem in the future will more likely do so than a student without a plan. The essay assignment provides a means for this to happen, along with a starting point to discuss other possible options for problem resolution.

Strategy: Form a Smart Discipline Support Group

Instructions: If your school already has a Smart Discipline support group for teachers, present your problem student to the group and brainstorm solutions.

> **Note:** If your school does not have a Smart Discipline support group, start one. You will be doing yourself, other teachers, and lots of students a big favor.

Seek out strategies that other teachers have used successfully with this particular student. Find out what other approaches different teachers have used successfully with similar students.

For best results, use the Smart Discipline Problem Analysis and Plan of Action form on pages 71 to 72 of this chapter to present to your problem student. Although it can be beneficial to use this forum to vent your frustration, be sure you come away with several concrete suggestions that you would feel comfortable using.

For additional information on how to start a Smart Discipline support group, call my office at 1-800-208-0807. Ask at the same time about the *Smart Discipline Magazine*.

Strategy: Consult With Principal and Counselor

Instructions: Set up a meeting between yourself, the principal, and the school counselor. Present your documentation of the student's behavior and your actions to date. Brainstorm and set up a plan of action.

> ***Note:*** Make this a formal meeting, not a hasty discussion on the run. Document what was talked about and agreed on.

For the most part, meetings with the principal and counselor will come after trying numerous other strategies without achieving positive results. However, there are some exceptions. You will want to consult with the principal immediately in the following cases:

- Evidence of suspicion of abuse
- Evidence or threats of violence
- Evidence of suicide attempts or threats

Make a verbal report immediately. It is a good idea to follow up with a brief written report of which you keep a copy.

Strategy: Schedule a Meeting With the Principal, Counselor, Parents, Student, and Yourself

Instructions: Accomplish the following three things at this meeting:

1. Agree on setting up an evaluation for the student with the school psychologist.

2. Agree on behaviors that will cause suspension. If possible, arrange for in-house suspension.

3. Ask parents to coordinate consequences at home with behavior at school. Suggest use of the Smart Discipline tracking charts. (See pages 46 to 47; you may make photocopies of these.)

> **Note:** Both the student and the parents need to get the idea from this meeting that (a) further misconduct of the type discussed will result in suspension, and (b) the school desires to provide the help necessary for the student to be successful.

By the time things progress to this event, the prognosis is usually not very good. Sometimes, a meeting like this can get a student in touch with the help he or she needs to turn the situation around. With some students, it may make the difference between their ending up in college or in prison.

What a joy it is to take part in helping a student turn away from a path of self-destruction. It is worth every bit of effort that you have to put into the process!

Please note: Review the Plan B strategies that you feel comfortable with and make note of them on your Smart Discipline Plan on page 96.

SMART DISCIPLINE

Problem Analysis and Plan of Action

Student's Name: _____ Date: _____

Teacher's Name: _____ Class: _____

1. List the student's most frequent problem behaviors.

    a. _____

    b. _____

    c. _____

    d. _____

    e. _____

    f. _____

2. List the desired behaviors.

    a. _____

    b. _____

    c. _____

    d. _____

    e. _____

    f. _____

3. List strategies that have been tried.

    a. _____

    b. _____

    c. _____

    d. _____

    e. _____

    f. _____

(Continued)

(Continued)

4. List strategies that work with this student.

   a. _____

   b. _____

   c. _____

   d. _____

5. List strategies that have not been successful.

   a. _____

   b. _____

   c. _____

6. List three strategies to try next.

   a. _____

   b. _____

   c. _____

Attention Deficit Hyperactivity Disorder Strategies 8

Before getting into the strategies that work for students with ADHD, review the following points.

1. ADHD is marked by (a) impulsivity, (b) inattention, and (c) hyperactivity (fast-paced activity without a purpose). Children with the condition normally are restless, are easily distracted, show poor judgment, and have poor social skills.

2. Students with ADHD often have low self-esteem as a result of the constant negative feedback that their behavior draws to them.

3. Bad parenting does not cause ADHD. This is a common myth. Although the causes remain unknown, it cannot be attributed to mistakes in parenting techniques (lots of parents of ADHD children have other highly successful children with normal behavior).

4. ADHD children can change. It takes longer and is more difficult, but normal behavior is within their grasp. Most will need assistance to attain it as their internal controls are underdeveloped. Until they develop, external controls must be provided.

5. Students with ADHD often are very good at escaping from work and consequences for their behavior. Frequently, they are allowed to skate out from under work assignments or consequences because of their disability. This sets up an unfortunate pattern of irresponsibility. Patterns like this can be reversed, but it takes time; effort; and, most of all, loads of patience in implementing a well-thought-out plan of action.

6. Established routines help children with ADHD control their behavior. The more predictable their day, the better off they are. Conversely, unpredictability is upsetting to them.

7. ADHD kids need a structured set of rules and consequences. The rules need to be consistently enforced with immediate consequences. Providing this kind of structure and predictability greatly improves the chances of a child's learning to control his or her behavior.

8. ADHD kids are less sensitive to rewards and consequences; therefore, bigger rewards and consequences need to be used. A slower response time can also be expected. More time, effort, and persistence will be needed to respond to a structured system of discipline.

9. When working with an ADHD child, it is possible to work effectively only with one or possibly two behaviors at a time. Trying to change more than this will only result in frustration and failure.

10. Overt reprimands agitate kids with ADHD. In fact, they cause a child to act out further. They respond far more positively to covert reminders and messages about consequences and time-outs.

11. As with any child, behavior is more successfully controlled if the child can expect consequences to be enforced at home as well as at school. An ideal format for accomplishing this is the Smart Discipline charting system, as described in Chapter 5. Communication between school and home will have to occur daily. However, the effort will pay off in much more controlled and productive behavior.

12. Until an ADHD child's behavior is under control, you can expect very little schoolwork or learning to take place. Therefore, priority one is a plan of action to help the child learn how to control his or her behavior. In the meantime, do not set high goals for the output and quality of schoolwork. Doing so will only frustrate you and the child.

13. Do not label a child as having ADHD. Misdiagnosis can cause a child not to receive proper treatment for other possible conditions. Also, the diagnosis of ADHD can be highly upsetting to parents and needs to be dealt with in a professional setting by a physician or mental health professional.

14. Biological intervention with methylphenidate (trade name, Ritalin) helps some children with ADHD become less impulsive, less hyper, and more attentive. However, it is not a cure-all. Ritalin cannot be expected to motivate a child to do his or her schoolwork and to follow the rules. This will still have to be done through working closely with the child, addressing one behavior at a time.

15. Kids with ADHD take great pride in learning how to control their behavior and in achieving goals. And it is a great joy to help them do so.

16. The major goals of working with ADHD students are to get them to think before they act and to control their own behavior. Achieving this

takes longer than it does with other kids. However, you can get 80 percent of the way there with the strategies described in other chapters of this book. The other 20 percent, given time, patience, and persistence, can be achieved with the following strategies.

Strategy: Choose Close Proximity

Instructions: Choose a seat as close to you as possible for the ADHD student.

> **Note:** Having the child close to you means you will spend less time responding to his or her behavior. Also, it allows you to easily teach from the child's "space," which helps with behavior control. As with any student, the behavior of students who are sitting close to the teacher is normally better than those who are sitting farther away (at least for kids prone to misbehaving).

Strategy: Set a Desired Behavior

Instructions: Pick out the single behavior that is bothering you the most. Decide what behavior you want instead. Choose three strategies from this chapter and previous chapters that you could use to prompt the desired behavior. Write them down.

Examples:

1. Unwanted behavior: Wandering out of seat

2. Desired behavior: To stay in seat unless the child raises hand for permission to be out of seat

3. Strategies to try:
   a. Write a note
   b. Implement four-step time-out (see page 78)
   c. Show appreciation

> **Note:** Remember not to expect immediate results. In fact, you can expect sporadic compliance that will improve over time. Resist the urge to give up and try something else. Stick with your plan for four weeks. At that time, assess what worked and what did not. Then, keep what did work, and change the rest.

Strategy: Use Smart Discipline Chart

Instructions: Same as described under the Smart Discipline System in Chapter 5. Modify the system to include only one or two rules. When those are consistently being followed, add another one.

> **Note:** If possible, encourage the parent to provide a consequence at home if all of the squares are lost at school. These consequences might include such things as
>
> 1. Loss of TV time
> 2. Loss of outside play time
> 3. Loss of bike privileges
> 4. Earlier bedtime
> 5. Loss of electronic game playing time
> 6. Extra chores

If interested in further information, the parent may want to order the *Smart Discipline Workbook* (which describes all of the steps of this system for the home) by calling 1-800-208-0807.

With ADHD students especially, be sure to fill in the blank provided for "Good Job Yesterday on." Ample amounts of encouragement are just as beneficial as providing a solid structure of rules and consequences.

Strategy: Give Covert Reminders

Instructions: When you observe an ADHD student starting into an unacceptable behavior, instead of a harsh reprimand, give a friendly reminder to help the student think before he or she acts.

Examples:

- "Jimmy, do you think that's wise?"
- "Brenda, remember what we talked about?"
- "Kyle, what is the rule?"
- "Jan, what is the consequence for that?"

> **Note:** Be sure to smile and respond by saying, "Good thinking" when the student responds positively to your reminder. The purpose, of course, is to help a child to think before he or she acts and for the child to control his or her own behavior. Because they are different from other kids, many, many more reminders will have to be given to achieve results.

Remember here also that harsh reprimands only aggravate the situation. Although it is tough sometimes not to react angrily to a child's repetitive misbehaviors, the consequence of expressing that anger is to cause further misbehavior. What works are friendly, covert reminders.

Rules should be short, simple, and specific.

Strategy: Encourage Afterschool Activities

Instructions: Encourage the student to participate in afterschool activities, such as Scouts, sports, music, art, and drama programs.

> *Note:* Many children like these activities enough that they will strive very hard to learn to control their behavior in order to participate. Also of benefit are the social skills learned and the insight reached through feedback given by peers.

Strategy: Implement Four-Step Time-Out

Instructions:

Step 1: Set up four different places to send students for time-out, such as

    a. In the classroom but separate from the rest of the class

    b. In the hallway or another teacher's class

    c. In a special chair in the principal's office

    d. In the student's home

Step 2: Explain to the student what behavior will cause him or her to be sent to time-out. Use only one or two behaviors at a time (pick the most disruptive behaviors first).

Step 3: Explain to the student that the first offense will result in an in-class time-out, the second offense in a hallway time-out, and so on.

Step 4: Ask the parents if they would be willing to pick up their child and put him or her in time-out at home. If this is not possible, brainstorm with the principal on possible alternatives.

> *Note:* One objection to taking children out of the classroom is that they will not be learning anything. In response to this objection, it should be noted that children are not learning anything while disrupting the class, either. At least by taking them out of the classroom, they are learning that if they break the rule, they will not be allowed to participate with the rest of the class.

Follow through with as much consistency as possible. Do not give a warning once an offense has occurred (unless the child is on a Smart Discipline chart with one of the consequences being a time-out. In this case, he or she has three free chances or warnings built into the system). However, if you observe the student starting into a misbehavior, you may want to use a covert reminder to help the child stop himself or herself from breaking the rules.

If the child refuses to move to time-out, say, "I see you decided to stay here. We'll talk about it later." Later, talk about it and impose a consequence like the loss of the next recess. Explain that the same thing will happen if he or she refuses time-out in the future.

Strategy: Respond With One-Liners

Instructions: Respond to repetitive questions and statements with one-liners. Use them repetitively.

Examples:

Student: When are we going to have our party?
Teacher: When did I tell you?

Student: That's not fair!
Teacher: Probably so.

Student: Can I _____?
Teacher: Let me think about it.

Student: Is it lunchtime yet?
Teacher: You tell me.

> *Note:* Say it in a friendly, caring way so you do not come off as being sarcastic. The purpose of this strategy is not to fall into the trap of reinforcing children's repetitive questions by giving them your attention. If you stick with the same one-liners each time, eventually, children will stop asking repetitive questions. Be prepared, though, for it to take a while.

Strategy: Refocus

Instructions: Make a list of at least five desirable behaviors and traits that the child displays. In a private way, let the child know you noticed his or her positive behavior or trait.

Sample List:

1. Punctual
2. Creative
3. Friendly

4. Truthful

5. Intelligent

Sample Statements:

1. "John, I noticed you were on time again today. Good job."

2. "Sally, let me tell you what I like about your poster." (Describe what you like.)

3. "Bobby, I noticed you made friends with the new student. That was nice of you."

4. "Craig, I like the way you tell the truth."

5. "Bonnie, you remembered all of the state capitals. You have a good memory."

Note: Sadly, people who work with ADHD children often get so focused on the "bad behavior" that these children get negative feedback literally heaped on them. As this happens, their self-concept worsens, as does their behavior. Lucky is the student who has a teacher willing to take the time and effort to notice and focus on the positive. Their self-concept improves, as does their behavior.

To make your encouragement meaningful, make sure to attach it to evidence. Also, in order not to reinforce some children's addiction to attention, give your positive feedback in private. And if the child is fishing for praise, respond with statements such as, "Tell me what you like about your project (or performance)."

If the child responds negatively or with a "poor me" attitude, resist the urge to talk the child out of it or to point out the positive. Instead, allow the child to have his or her feeling or thought by simply restating the thought or clarifying the feeling, for example, "Sounds like you are dissatisfied with your poster, is that right?" or "It seems like you are angry with yourself, is that right?"

Strategy: Consult With Former Teachers

Instructions: Seek out former teachers and ask what they found worked with a particular student and what did not.

Consult also with other teachers the student may currently have. Some children with ADHD respond incredibly well to certain teachers. You will want to explore what this teacher is doing differently.

Note: Beware of the response, "Nothing works with him." If questioned further, most teachers will remember a few things that seemed to work better than others. If not, it does not mean that nothing works. Rather, it means that what works has not yet been found or tried with this particular child.

Strategy: Analyze Achievement

Instructions: When a child sometimes behaves appropriately and sometimes does not, see if you can figure out the difference in the conditions that might possibly be influencing the child's choices of behavior. Consider the following in relation to times he or she was behaving, as opposed to misbehaving:

1. Were you saying or doing anything differently?
2. What were the noise and activity levels in the class?
3. What were the times of day?
4. What were the days of the week?
5. What activities preceded the behavior?
6. What activities were coming up that day?

Note: Repeat this exercise and document your answers over a four-week period. See if any patterns seem to emerge. If possible, question parents about periods of marked good or bad behavior. Get their thoughts as to what might be possible causes.

You will want, of course, to modify conditions that seem to adversely affect behavior and repeat the variables that foster good behavior.

The common objection to this process is time. Teachers say, "I don't have the time for this. I have 30 other kids to teach." They are right, and only the ones who lose enough time from teaching due to disruptive ADHD behavior will be motivated to take the necessary time and effort to implement this strategy.

Strategy: Physical Contact

Instructions: Try making physical contact by

1. Handshakes
2. Pats on the arm or back
3. Resting a hand on the student's shoulder while teaching

> *Note:* With some children, touching can create a powerful bond between teacher and student. With the creation of this bond comes a huge desire on the student's part to cooperate with the teacher.

Other students with ADHD may react negatively to touching. If so, do not force it, simply move on to another strategy.

Strategy: Slow Tempo

Instructions: When responding to a child displaying hyperactive behavior, speak very calmly, slowly, and softly.

> *Note:* Your slower and calmer speech pattern will tend to help the child slow and calm down. This is often tough to do because the natural response to hyperactivity is to loudly and quickly react to the child. This only reinforces the hyperactivity.

Slowing your tempo gives a child more time to think about what he or she is saying and doing. And if nothing else, it will allow you to stay calm!

Strategy: Assign Predictable Responsibilities

Instructions: Brainstorm chores that need to be done daily in your classroom or school. Ask the child if he or she would help you out by taking on the responsibility of completing that task at a certain time each day.

> *Note:* Make sure to show the student exactly what needs to be done so that the child virtually cannot fail. Do not assign meaningless tasks, but rather, assign ones where the student can feel he or she is making an important contribution.

Although it is often easier to do tasks yourself, you do the ADHD child a big favor by assigning predictable responsibilities. First, it helps a child foster a belief that he or she "has what it takes to be successful." Second, children with ADHD do better when their day is structured and predictable.

Let the parents know what you are doing and why. The possible perception that you are "making the child work" must be avoided.

Strategy: Facilitate Insights

Instructions: When you notice the student displaying the desired behavior, set aside time to ask the student how he or she was able to control that behavior. Also, ask what was done differently.

Note: If the child responds with, "I don't know," give the child some choices, such as

- "Phillip, I noticed you stayed in your seat today. How did you do that?"
- "Well, was it because you were stuck to your chair or because you decided to stay in it?"
- "Casey, I noticed that you didn't get into any fights on the playground. What did you do differently today?"
- "Do you think you didn't fight today because you forgot how or because you decided to do other things instead?"

Be sure to make one choice absurd and one that helps point out that the child is in control of his or her behavior. This conversation should be private but can be accomplished without taking much time by limiting it to just a few seconds.

Strategy: Organize a Conference

Instructions: Enlist the school counselor's help in setting up a conference to include all teachers presently working with the child, the parents, the school psychologist, and the principal, if appropriate.

Note: The purpose of this conference should be to set up an action plan that includes recommendations for appropriate evaluations and referrals to community and school resources. Stay away from blame and labels. Direct all efforts to the delineation of an action plan complete with timeline, assignment or tasks, and method of follow-up.

Please note: Pick out the ADHD strategies that you can make use of and note them in your personal Smart Discipline Plan under "ADHD Strategies." Be sure to include other strategies that you have found to be effective with ADHD students.

Suggest a structured time for homework.

Parental Support and Involvement 9

Parents are important. If you have their support, the tasks of both teaching and discipline go much better. In all the current research, parental support and involvement has been found to be the number one factor affecting success in school (Hoover-Dempsey & Sandler, 1995). Simply stated, if a parent is involved in the student's education, the chances of the child being successful in the classroom are far greater than those of a student whose parents are not involved.

Today's students have parents who fall into three basic categories when it comes to involvement with the education process. First, there are the highly active parents who are closely involved with every aspect of their child's education. Second, there are the parents who certainly care about their child's education but do not take much of an active role in the process unless there are problems. The third group of parents is comprised of parents who, for a variety of reasons, are not involved at any level in their child's education.

Dealing with the first group of parents offers few challenges. Normally, their children are well behaved, and when they do misbehave, a call to the parents is all that it takes to straighten the situation out. A few of these very active parents can be overbearing, and the strategies in this chapter will help you deal effectively with them.

The second group is a very large group of parents and is a group that, given the right direction by the teacher, can make a big difference in the level of cooperation of their children at school. These parents are very reachable, and it is these parents from whom the strategies in this chapter will help you gain active support.

Even parents who seem to care less about their children's education can sometimes be turned around. It can be well worth the effort to try a few of these strategies with them to see if you can draw them in to help support you in gaining their child's cooperation. Where others have failed to reach them, you just might be the person to whom they will respond.

One final note I would like to make before presenting the strategies for parental involvement and support is that there was a time that these actions, for the most part, were not necessary. Parents supported teachers automatically. Children knew full well that if they got into trouble at school, they would be in even bigger trouble at home. Thus, behavior at school was far better than it is today. Although it is not probable that we will return to that idyllic situation any time soon, it is certainly possible to help garner this kind of support from most parents on an individual basis. It takes some effort, but if it works, it is well worth it. Doing so can make the difference between a child deciding to fully cooperate with you and not cooperating in the slightest.

Strategy: Establish Classroom Rules, Consequences, and Rewards

Instructions: Write out your five most important classroom rules and the consequences for breaking the rules. Add to this a list of five ways that you will reward positive behavior.

Note: Parents judge a teacher's competency on the basis of these four things: ability to discipline, desire to work with parents, organizational skills, and willingness to balance negative feedback with positive feedback. This makes sense because competent teachers normally exhibit each of these characteristics. Therefore, to gain parents' support, it is essential to show them clearly that you have these attributes.

Sample Rules:

1. Speak with respect to teacher and classmates.
2. Raise your hand for permission to speak.
3. Stay at your seat unless you have permission to move.
4. Walk, do not run.
5. Have homework done neatly and on time.

Sample Consequences:

1. Loss of first half of recess
2. Loss of all of recess
3. Time-out in hallway
4. Time-out in principal's office
5. Stay after school in detention room

Sample Rewards:

1. Praise
2. Teacher's helper for the day

3. Note sent home to parents

4. Note to principal

5. Special treats and activities

Strategy: Communicate With Parents

Instructions: Write a letter to all of the parents of your students that communicates your desire to work together with them to ensure that their child is successful in your class. Include in the letter your rules, consequences, and rewards. You may also wish to communicate your philosophy of teaching and homework expectations. At the same time, be sure to request that the parents inform you of anything they think might be helpful for you to know about their child.

Sample Letter:

Dear Parents:

I want to introduce myself and let you know that I am pleased to have your child in my class this year. It is very important to me that each child I teach is successful in my class. Because parental support and involvement are the most important factors in a child's success at school, I want to support your involvement in your child's education in every way that I can.

First, I think it would be helpful for you to know the top five most important rules in my classroom. They include the following: (1) speak with respect to teacher and classmates; (2) raise your hand for permission to speak; (3) stay at your seat unless you have permission to move; (4) walk, do not run; and (5) have homework done neatly and on time.

The consequences for breaking the rules are as follows:

First offense:	Warning
Second offense:	Loss of half of recess
Third offense:	Loss of whole recess
Fourth offense:	Time-out in principal's office
Fifth offense:	Stay after school in detention room

Please note that every day, each child starts over with a clean slate. Rewards for positive behavior include the following:

1. Praise
2. Teacher's helper for the day
3. Note home to parents
4. Note to principal
5. Special treats and activities

You can expect that I will communicate with you about not only your child's behaviors, both positive and negative, but also your child's academic progress. At the same time, I invite you to communicate with

---

me (I would especially appreciate it if you would tell me of any special problems that your child might have that could affect his performance in school).

Please feel free to contact me in any of the following ways. You can leave a phone message for me at the school, and I will call you back as soon as I can. The number at the school is 555-4359. You can also write to me in care of the school. The address is Ms. Barnesworth, Blaine Elementary, 1234 Cedar Lane, Anytown, WI 53805. You can also e-mail me at Msbarnesworth@blainelementary.org.

Again, I thank you for your support, and I look forward to working with you.

Sincerely,
Bobbi Barnesworth
Third-grade teacher

Note: You can either send this letter to the parents or make copies and go over it with them at an open house meeting. Sending, I think, is preferable because parents are likely to read the letter and take it seriously. By sending it, you are also more likely to reach a greater percentage of the parents. Once you have communicated the above, most parents will get the message that you are serious about classroom discipline, have a desire to work with parents, are organized, and are fair-minded.

Strategy: Report Good Behavior to Parents

Instructions: Each week, pick out at least two students to focus on. Observe them, and document one or two positive behaviors from each of them. Write a short note home to their parents about the positive behavior. Keep the note 100 percent positive.

Note: Many teachers say that they do not have the time for this. However, this is one of those activities that is truly a good investment. Not only will you get great feedback from the parents, but also each time you send a note home, you will increase the likelihood of that child cooperating with you in your classroom. As a rule of thumb, pick one child each week for this who is one of your more difficult children to deal with. These are the parents and the student for which this strategy has the greatest potential to help you gain their cooperation.

Sample Letter:

Dear Mr. and Mrs. Smythe:

I want you to know that I enjoy having your daughter Karen in my class. Here are a couple of examples as to why. Just this week, she went out of her way to help me carry some things into the classroom. She also handed her homework in on time. In addition, she was very cooperative this week. You have much to be proud of!

Sincerely,
Ms. Barnes

Strategy: Document Problem Behaviors

Instructions: In a notebook, start pages for each student with the student's name at the top. For each misbehavior, write down the date and time, describe the behavior, and make note of the action you took.

Sample Documentation:

Tory Williams

October 20	At 12:15, I saw Tory spit at Cindy. I gave him a warning.
October 20	At 12:35, Tory kicked Jason. I took away half of his recess.
October 21	At 9:20, Tory got out of his seat and rolled his eyes at me when I asked him to sit down. I warned him.
October 21	At 9:45, Tory threw a paper wad across the room. I took away half of his recess.
October 21	At 10:15, Tory shoved Brian's books off his desk. I took away the other half of his recess.
October 21	At 11:30, Tory threw food in the cafeteria. I sent him to the office for a 30-minute time-out.
October 21	At 1:25, Tory tore up Cindy's notebook. I told Tory he would have to stay after school tomorrow. I will call his parents this evening and discuss the situation with them.

Note: Keep in mind that although doing this may seem like a lot of work, it is absolutely essential to have documentation if you are to deal effectively with parents or with possible referral sources. If you have this kind of documentation, your credibility will be very high, and this will strengthen the chances of getting the kind of support you need to turn any given student's misbehavior around. Having documentation will also bolster your confidence when dealing with the parents.

Strategy: Set Up a Parent Conference

Instructions: At the point when you see that your normal disciplinary strategies are not working with a student, call the parents in for a conference. In advance of the conference, make sure to have

- Clear documentation of the misbehavior
- The goal of the conference written down
- Several ideas written down about what the parents can do to help
- The possible benefits of the parents taking action
- Possible consequences of the situation not being handled effectively

Hold the parent conference. Start out with some positive observations about the parent's child. Praise the parent for taking the time and effort to meet with you. Then, go over the record of the misbehavior and the actions you have taken thus far. Suggest some ways the parents might help. Make sure to also ask them what they think they might do to help motivate their child to cooperate at school. State the benefits of taking action. Predict possible consequences if effective action is not taken. Clarify and write down a plan of action stating both what action the parents will take and what actions you will take. End the conference on a positive, upbeat note.

Sample Parent Conference:

Ms. Barnesworth: Thank you for taking the time and effort to come in. Having your support makes a great deal of difference to me, and it is sure to help your son as well. Let me first start by saying that there are many good things about your son's behavior and academic progress. He does very well in arithmetic and loves to volunteer whenever I need help.

Mr. Smythe: So, then what's the problem?

Ms. Barnesworth: Well, let me show you. I keep a record of students' misbehavior and the action I took at the time. As you can see from Tory's record, he has been disruptive in my class on a number of occasions. And despite my normal actions, Tory continues to misbehave. However, I think that if we work together, we can remedy the situation.

Mr. Smythe: I don't understand it. I told him he better straighten up or he was going to be in big trouble.

Ms. Barnesworth: Let's look at some things parents can do in this situation that have a record of being effective. As I go over them, feel free to interject any ideas that you might have that could work as well.

Mr. Smythe:	I'll be happy to listen, but to tell you the truth, Tory acts up at home too, and nothing we do seems to help.
Ms. Barnesworth:	Perhaps together we can come up with something that will work. One way that oftentimes works is when I have the student take a report home each day on his misbehavior. The parents in turn take away a privilege for each time their child misbehaved that day. How does that sound to you?
Mr. Smythe:	That sounds like a hassle. Can't you just handle this at school? Maybe have the principal spank him if he's bad?
Ms. Barnesworth:	That would be great, if we could handle it all at school, wouldn't it? And yes, it is a lot of work to get some children to behave at school, but it's worth it. If you can help me get Tory to behave, he will pass the third grade and will learn the things he will need for the fourth grade.
Mr. Smythe:	Are you saying Tory might flunk? I didn't think the situation was that bad.
Ms. Barnesworth:	Yes, if he continues to be disruptive, he will likely miss the things he needs to learn, and if he flunks, I will have no choice but to keep him back.
Mr. Smythe:	Tell me again what you want us to do.
Ms. Barnesworth:	Two things. First make a list of privileges that you will take away if Tory misbehaves at school. Second, make a list of small rewards that you will give him if he behaves at school.
Mr. Smythe:	What kinds of things are you talking about?
Ms. Barnesworth:	Here's a list. The list of privileges might include things like watching favorite television programs, staying up until his normal bedtime, going outside to play, having playtime with his friends, riding his bike, or playing with favorite toys. Rewards may include things like praise, stickers, special treats or activities, and weekend activities.
Mr. Smythe:	Are you sure this will work?
Ms. Barnesworth:	It works with many children. The major factor in its success is persistence. For it to have a good chance of working, you will have to keep to it until we all agree that the situation has been rectified. Are you willing to make that kind of commitment?

Mr. Smythe: I suppose we'll have to do it.

Ms. Barnesworth: Great! I'll make note of your commitment in Tory's record along with a note of my commitment to sending a report home every day about his behavior, both good and bad. I can't thank you enough for supporting me. It will likely make the difference between Tory passing or flunking the third grade.

Note: The biggest mistakes teachers make in holding parent conferences include waiting too long to inform the parents of the problems, not being prepared for the conference, and not pushing for a commitment to a specific plan of action. If you take advantage of the strategies in this chapter, you will not fall victim to these mistakes.

However, you may well encounter some highly uncooperative parents who may refuse to comply, blame the problem on you or the school, or otherwise blow you off in a variety of ways. The very best way to respond to these parents is by being positive, upbeat, enthusiastic, and assertive all at the same time. Do not allow yourself the luxury of being negative in any fashion. It will only serve to fuel the flames of their anger and defensiveness. If at all possible, let their negativity fuel your positive enthusiasm. Doing so may well serve to turn their attitude totally around.

Your Personal Smart Discipline Plan 10

The major purpose of this book is to provide numerous positive discipline strategies from which a teacher can pick and choose to design a personal Smart Discipline Plan. To pull a comprehensive personal plan together, choose from all four categories: (1) prevention strategies, (2) Plan A strategies, (3) Plan B strategies, and (d) ADHD strategies.

A quick reference guide is on the next six pages. Check off the strategies that align with your teaching style, and note them on your personal Smart Discipline Plan on pages 98 and 99. Make sure also to note other strategies that have worked for you and other teachers in the past.

As you fill out your plan, first complete the section provided for the misbehaviors you most frequently encounter, along with the behaviors you have the most difficulty correcting. As you pick out the different strategies to include in your plan, make sure they address these behaviors.

For best results, try out one strategy at a time. Once that one is consistently working for you, try out another one. By doing this, your Smart Discipline strategies will become second nature to you. And best of all, you will become a master of classroom discipline. I guarantee it!

PREVENTION STRATEGIES

Check off those that appeal to you, and list them on page 98.

- ❑ Welcome students (page 28)

- ❑ Express appreciation (page 28)

- ❑ Write a note (page 30)

- ❑ Write a letter (page 30)

- ❑ Call home (page 31)

- ❑ Ask personal questions (page 32)

- ❑ Transpose critical comments (page 32)

- ❑ Point out talents (page 33)

- ❑ Predict success (page 34)

- ❑ Make appointments (page 35)

- ❑ Elicit third-party encouragement (page 37)

- ❑ List misplaced behaviors (page 38)

PLAN A STRATEGIES

Check off those that appeal to you, and list them on page 99.

- ❑ Use friendly evil eye (page 49)

- ❑ Invade space (page 50)

- ❑ Touch shoulder (page 50)

- ❑ Whisper technique (page 50)

- ❑ Smile and request (page 51)

- ❑ Allow thinking time (page 51)

- ❑ Change locations (page 52)

- ❑ Exercise the quiet signal (page 52)

- ❑ State your want (page 53)

- ❑ Give information (page 53)

- ❑ Convey qualities plus expectations (page 53)

- ❑ Give choices (page 54)

- ❑ Respect the struggle (page 55)

- ❑ Answer questions with questions (page 55)

- ❑ Do research (page 56)

PLAN B STRATEGIES

Check off those that appeal to you, and list them on page 99.

- ❑ Write a note (page 58)

- ❑ Express strong feelings (page 58)

- ❑ Arrange mini-counseling session (page 60)

- ❑ Schedule cooperative planning session (page 60)

- ❑ Chart behavior and consequences (page 61)

- ❑ Use time-out (page 61)

- ❑ Change volume and tempo (page 62)

- ❑ Encourage student involvement (page 62)

- ❑ Build relationships (page 63)

- ❑ Use activities for leverage (page 64)

- ❑ Analyze and plan (page 65)

- ❑ Inform parents (page 65)

- ❑ Give responsibilities (page 65)

- ❑ Encourage involvement (page 66)

- ❑ Plan for amends (page 66)

- ❑ Deliver "I" messages (page 67)

- ❑ Assign student essay (page 68)

- ❑ Form a Smart Discipline support group (page 68)

- ❑ Consult with principal and counselor (page 69)

- ❑ Schedule a meeting with the principal, counselor, parents, student, and yourself (page 69)

ADHD STRATEGIES

Check off those that appeal to you, and list them on page 99.

- ❏ Choose close proximity (page 75)

- ❏ Set a desired behavior (page 75)

- ❏ Use Smart Discipline chart (page 76)

- ❏ Give covert reminders (page 76)

- ❏ Encourage afterschool activities (page 77)

- ❏ Implement four-step time-out (page 78)

- ❏ Respond with one-liners (page 79)

- ❏ Refocus (page 79)

- ❏ Consult with former teachers (page 80)

- ❏ Analyze achievement (page 81)

- ❏ Physical contact (page 81)

- ❏ Slow tempo (page 82)

- ❏ Assign predictable responsibilities (page 82)

- ❏ Facilitate insights (page 83)

- ❏ Organize a conference (page 83)

SMART DISCIPLINE PLAN

Teacher's Name: _____   Date: _____

List the five most frequent misbehaviors you encounter in your class. After you fill out the rest of your plan, come back and fill in "Strategies to Use."

Behaviors	*Strategies to Use*
1. _____	_____
2. _____	_____
3. _____	_____
4. _____	_____
5. _____	_____

List the three behaviors that are the most difficult for you to correct. As above, fill in the "Strategies to Use" after filling out the rest of your plan.

Behaviors	*Strategies to Use*
1. _____	_____
2. _____	_____
3. _____	_____

List below the prevention strategies that appeal to you most. Add any reminders or notes.

Prevention Strategies	*Notes and Reminders*
1. _____	_____
2. _____	_____
3. _____	_____
4. _____	_____
5. _____	_____
6. _____	_____
7. _____	_____
8. _____	_____
9. _____	_____
10. _____	_____

List your Plan A strategies here with notes and reminders. Be sure to add other strategies that have worked in the past, either for you or for other teachers.

Plan A Strategies	*Notes and Reminders*
1. _____	_____
2. _____	_____
3. _____	_____
4. _____	_____
5. _____	_____

List below the Plan B strategies you can use. Add to the list suggestions from other teachers, as well as ideas from your own experience.

Plan B Strategies	*Notes and Reminders*
1. _____	_____
2. _____	_____
3. _____	_____
4. _____	_____
5. _____	_____

List here the ADHD strategies that make sense to you. Include anything and everything that might work.

ADHD Strategies	*Notes and Reminders*
1. _____	_____
2. _____	_____
3. _____	_____
4. _____	_____
5. _____	_____

Please note: Remember to go back to your list of the most frequent and difficult behaviors you encounter and fill in the blanks for "Strategies to Use."

Note From the Author

We invite you to participate in ongoing research about the effectiveness of the Smart Discipline system. Please select from the following questionnaires as appropriate and return completed forms to Nydia@smartdiscipline.com or visit www.smartdiscipline.com for our mailing address.

RESEARCH QUESTIONS FOR SMART DISCIPLINE FOR THE CLASSROOM

Questions for Teachers

Date: _____

Name: _____

Grade(s) Taught: _____ Number of Years as a Teacher: _____

Subjects Taught (if other than classroom teacher): _____

Name of School: _____

Address: _____

City/State/Zip: _____

E-mail Address: _____

Phone Number: _____ May we use you for a reference? _____

How many discipline referrals to the principal's office did you make the year prior to implementing the Smart Charts at your school? _____

How many discipline referrals to the principal's office did you make the year the Smart Charts were implemented at your school? _____ If this reflects a partial school year, please note how many months the Smart Charts were in use. _____

Please circle the best answer to the following questions:

Use of the Smart Charts helps enhance parent and teacher communication.

Strongly Agree   Agree   Disagree   Strongly Disagree   N/A

My time spent on discipline is reduced by the use of the Smart Charts.

Strongly Agree   Agree   Disagree   Strongly Disagree   N/A

Hallway behavior has gotten more orderly since implementing the Smart Charts.

Strongly Agree   Agree   Disagree   Strongly Disagree   N/A

Using the Smart Charts has helped create a better learning environment in my classroom.

Strongly Agree   Agree   Disagree   Strongly Disagree   N/A

I have noticed an improvement in playground behavior since implementing the Smart Charts.

Strongly Agree   *Agree*   *Disagree*   *Strongly Disagree*   *N/A*

Student academic performance has been positively impacted by the use of the Smart Charts.

Strongly Agree   *Agree*   *Disagree*   *Strongly Disagree*   *N/A*

I would recommend that our school continue to use the Smart Charts.

Strongly Agree   *Agree*   *Disagree*   *Strongly Disagree*   *N/A*

What I like best about using the Smart Charts with my students is:

_____

_____

_____

Please note any comments or suggestions for ways to improve the Smart Chart program:

_____

_____

_____

_____

RESEARCH QUESTIONS FOR SMART DISCIPLINE FOR THE CLASSROOM

Questions for Principals and Assistant Principals

Date: _____

Name: _____

Title: _____ Number of Years as a Principal: _____

Name of School: _____

Address: _____

City/State/Zip: _____

E-mail Address: _____

Phone Number: _____ May we use you for a reference? _____

How many discipline referrals to your office were made the year prior to implementing the Smart Charts at your school? _____

How many discipline referrals to your office were made the year the Smart Charts were implemented at your school? _____ If this reflects a partial school year, please note how many months the Smart Charts were in use. _____

How many suspensions occurred at your school over discipline issues the year before using the Smart Charts? _____

How many school suspensions occurred at your school the year the Smart Charts were implemented? _____ If this reflects a partial school year, please note how many months the Smart Charts were in use. _____

Please circle the best answer to the following questions:

The Smart Charts help reduce time spent on discipline issues by school administrative staff (including you).

Strongly Agree　　　　*Agree*　　　　*Disagree*　　　　*Strongly Disagree*　　　　*N/A*

The Smart Charts help reduce discipline conferences with parents.

Strongly Agree　　　　*Agree*　　　　*Disagree*　　　　*Strongly Disagree*　　　　*N/A*

Parent and teacher communication has been enhanced by use of the Smart Charts.

Strongly Agree　　　　*Agree*　　　　*Disagree*　　　　*Strongly Disagree*　　　　*N/A*

The time spent by my teachers on discipline issues has been reduced by the use of the Smart Charts.

Strongly Agree   *Agree*   *Disagree*   *Strongly Disagree*   *N/A*

Hallway behavior has gotten more orderly since implementing the Smart Charts.

Strongly Agree   *Agree*   *Disagree*   *Strongly Disagree*   *N/A*

Using the Smart Charts creates a better learning environment in the classroom.

Strongly Agree   *Agree*   *Disagree*   *Strongly Disagree*   *N/A*

I have noticed an improvement in playground behavior since implementing the Smart Charts.

Strongly Agree   *Agree*   *Disagree*   *Strongly Disagree*   *N/A*

Student academic performance has been positively impacted by the use of the Smart Charts.

Strongly Agree   *Agree*   *Disagree*   *Strongly Disagree*   *N/A*

I would recommend that our school continue to use the Smart Charts.

Strongly Agree   *Agree*   *Disagree*   *Strongly Disagree*   *N/A*

What I like best about using the Smart Charts at our school is:

_____

_____

Please note any comments or suggestions for ways to improve the Smart Chart program:

_____

_____

_____

RESEARCH QUESTIONS FOR SMART DISCIPLINE FOR THE CLASSROOM

Questions for School Counselors and School Psychologists

Date: _____

Name: _____

Title: _____

Grades Responsible for: _____

Name of School: _____

Address: _____

City/State/Zip: _____

E-mail Address: _____

Phone Number: _____ May we use you for a reference? _____

How many discipline referrals were made to your office the year prior to implementing the Smart Charts at your school? _____

How many discipline referrals were made to your office the year Smart Charts were implemented at your school? _____ If this reflects a partial school year, please note how many months the Smart Charts were in use. _____

Please circle the best answer to the following questions:

Use of the Smart Charts helps enhance parent and teacher communication.

Strongly Agree　　　*Agree*　　　*Disagree*　　　*Strongly Disagree*　　　*N/A*

My time spent on discipline has been reduced by the use of the Smart Charts.

Strongly Agree　　　*Agree*　　　*Disagree*　　　*Strongly Disagree*　　　*N/A*

Hallway behavior has gotten more orderly since implementing the Smart Charts.

Strongly Agree　　　*Agree*　　　*Disagree*　　　*Strongly Disagree*　　　*N/A*

Use of the Smart Charts creates a better learning environment in the classrooms.

Strongly Agree　　　*Agree*　　　*Disagree*　　　*Strongly Disagree*　　　*N/A*

I have noticed an improvement in playground behavior since implementing the Smart Charts.

Strongly Agree   *Agree*   *Disagree*   *Strongly Disagree*   *N/A*

Student academic performance has been positively impacted by the use of the Smart Charts.

Strongly Agree   *Agree*   *Disagree*   *Strongly Disagree*   *N/A*

I would recommend that our school continue to use the Smart Charts.

Strongly Agree   *Agree*   *Disagree*   *Strongly Disagree*   *N/A*

What I like best about using the Smart Charts at this school is:

_____

_____

Please note any comments or suggestions for ways to improve the Smart Chart program:

_____

_____

_____

Suggested Readings

Anderson, J. (1981). *Thinking, changing, rearranging.* Portland, OR: Metamorphous.

Axelrod, S. (1977). *Behavior modification for the classroom teacher.* New York: McGraw-Hill.

Bartel, N., & Hammill, D. (1990). *Teaching students with learning and behavior problems* (5th ed.). Boston: Allyn & Bacon.

Baruth, L., & Eckstein, D. (1982). *The ABC's of classroom discipline.* Dubuque, IA: Randall/Hunt.

Bosch, K. (2006). *Planning classroom management.* Thousand Oaks, CA: Corwin Press.

Boynton, M., & Boynton, S. (2005). *The educator's guide to preventing and solving discipline problems.* Alexandria, VA: Association for Supervision and Curriculum Development.

Brophy, J. (1985). Classroom management as instruction: Socializing and self-guidance in students. *Theory Into Practice, 24,* 233–240.

Canter, L. (1984). *Lee Canter's parent conference book.* Santa Monica, CA: Lee Canter & Associates.

Charles, C. M. (1986). *Building classroom discipline from models to practice* (3rd ed.). White Plains, NY: Longman.

Cummings, C. (2000). *Winning strategies for classroom management.* Alexandria, VA: Association for Supervision and Curriculum Development.

Doyle, W. (1986). Classroom organization and management. In M. C. Wittrock (Ed.), *Handbook of research on teaching* (pp. 392–431). New York: Macmillan.

Dreikurs, R. (1982). *Maintaining sanity in the classroom.* New York: Harper & Row.

Dreikurs, R. (1991). *Discipline without tears.* New York: Plume.

Evertson, C. (1986). Training teachers in classroom management: An experimental study in secondary school classrooms. *Journal of Educational Research, 79,* 51–58.

Fifer, F. (1986). Effective classroom management. *Academic Therapy, 21,* 401–410.

Ginott, H. (1972). *Teacher and child: A book for parents and teachers.* New York: Avon.

Glasser, W. (1978). 10 steps to good discipline. *Today's Education, 66,* 60–63.

Glasser, W. (1986). *Control theory in the classroom.* New York: Harper & Row.

Glasser, W. (1990). *The quality school: Managing students without coercion.* New York: HarperPerennial.

Gordon, T. (1974). *Teacher effectiveness training.* New York: Wyden.

Hill, M. S., & Hill, F. W. (1994). *Creating safe schools: What principals can do.* Thousand Oaks, CA: Corwin Press.

Hoover-Dempsey, K., & Sandler, H. (1995). Parental involvement in children's education: Why does it make a difference? *Teachers College Record, 97*(2), 310–331.

Jones, F. (1979). The gentle art of classroom discipline. *National Elementary Principal, 58,* 26–30.

Jones, F. (1987). *Positive classroom discipline.* New York: McGraw-Hill.

Jones, F. (2000). *Tools for teaching.* Santa Cruz, CA: Fredric H. Jones & Associates.

Jones, V., & Jones, F. (1986). *Comprehensive classroom management* (2nd ed.). Boston: Allyn & Bacon.

Knitzer, J., Steinberg, Z., & Fleisch, B. (1990). *At the schoolhouse door: An examination of programs and policies for children with behavior and emotional problems.* New York: Bank Street College of Education.

Koenig, L. (2006). [*Smart Discipline for the Classroom* statistics]. Unpublished raw data.

Kottler, J. A. (2002). *Students who drive you crazy.* Thousand Oaks, CA: Corwin Press.

Kounin, J. (1977). *Discipline and group management in classrooms.* New York: Holt, Rinehart & Winston.

LaBelle, S. (2004). *Teaching smarter II.* Rochester, WA: Estarr Publishing.

Long, N. J., Morse, W. C., & Newman, R. G. (1980). *Conflict in the classroom: The education of children with problems* (4th ed.). Belmont, CA: Wadsworth.

Martin, R. (1980). *Teaching through encouragement.* Englewood Cliffs, NJ: Prentice Hall.

Marzano, R. (2003). *Classroom management that works.* Alexandria, VA: Association for Supervision and Curriculum Development.

McIntyre, T. (1989a). *A resource book for remediating common behavior and learning problems.* Boston: Allyn & Bacon.

McIntyre, T. (1989b). *The behavior management handbook: Setting up effective behavior management systems.* Boston: Allyn & Bacon.

McKay, M., & Fanning, P. (1986). *Self-esteem.* Oakland, CA: New Harbinger.

Mendler, A., & Curwin, R. (1999). *Discipline with dignity for challenging youth.* Bloomington, IN: National Education Service.

Nelson, J. (1999). *Positive time-out: And over 50 ways to avoid power struggles in the home and the classroom.* New York: Three Rivers Press.

O'Leary, D., & O'Leary, S. (1977). *Classroom management: The successful use of behavior modification* (2nd ed.). New York: Pergamon.

Podesta, C. (1990). *Self-esteem and the six-second secret.* Newbury Park, CA: Corwin Press.

Polsgrove, L. (1920). *Reducing undesirable behaviors.* Reston, VA: Council for Exceptional Children.

Quarles, C. L. (1993). *Staying safe at school.* Newbury Park, CA: Corwin Press.

Rardin, R. (1978, September). Classroom management made easy. *Virginia Journal of Education,* 14–17.

Rimm, S. B. (1986). *Underachievement syndrome: Causes and cures.* Watertown, WI: Apple.

Rizzo, J. V., & Zabel, R. H. (1988). *Educating children and adolescents with behavioral disorders: An integrative approach.* Boston: Allyn & Bacon.

Shevialkov, G., & Redd, F. (1956). *Discipline for today's children.* Washington, DC: Association for Supervision and Curriculum Development.

Short, P., Short, J., & Blanton, C. (1994). *Rethinking student discipline.* Thousand Oaks, CA: Corwin Press.

Simpson, R. L., Walker, B. L., Ormsbee, C. K., Downing, J. A., & Myles, B. S. (1991). *Programming for aggressive and violent students.* Reston, VA: ERIC.

Will, M. (1986). Educating children with learning problems: A shared responsibility. *Exceptional Children, 52,* 411–416.

Zionts, P. (1985). *Teaching disturbed and disturbing students: An integrative approach.* Austin, TX: Pro-Ed.

Index

CORWIN PRESS

The Corwin Press logo—a raven striding across an open book—represents the union of courage and learning. Corwin Press is committed to improving education for all learners by publishing books and other professional development resources for those serving the field of PreK–12 education. By providing practical, hands-on materials, Corwin Press continues to carry out the promise of its motto: **"Helping Educators Do Their Work Better."**